For a complete list of Management Books 2000 titles
visit our web-site on http://www.mb2000.com

MANAGEMENT BY FOOTBALL

Peter Kreilgaard, Daniel Soren and Henrik Sorensen

Danish edition first published 2008

This new English edition first published in 2010 by
Management Books 2000 Ltd
Forge House, Limes Road
Kemble, Cirencester
Gloucestershire, GL7 6AD, UK
Tel: 0044 (0) 1285 771441
Fax: 0044 (0) 1285 771055
Email: info@mb2000.com
Web: www.mb2000.com

British Library Cataloguing in Publication Data is available

ISBN 9781852526498

CONTENTS

INTRODUCTION

*"Some people believe football is a matter of life and death, I am very
disappointed with that attitude. I can assure you it is much, much
more important than that."*
Bill Shankly (1913-1981), www.liverpoolfc.tv

This world famous quote is as true today as the day it was stated by
former Manager of Liverpool, the late Bill Shankly. Football has in
every sense become a matter of life and death, metaphorically and
literally. For billions of people around the world football has
become part of everyday life and is a way of living. Football has the
ability to bring out the best and the worst in people. And it does.

Like a play by Shakespeare, football is a real time drama that
unfolds before our very eyes. It works at many levels and means
different things to different people. For some football is a sport that
entails great sportsmanship and physical agility. For others it is a
multibillion pound industry, employing thousands of people, with
giant-size contracts for sponsorships and TV rights. Players,
managers and owners are superstars, whose lives on and of the
pitch are followed by millions of people and hundreds of paparazzi.
For others again, football is the largest single sport in the world and
gives millions of people the opportunity to be part of a team,
building relationships, providing vital physical exercise and most
importantly tremendous joy. The popularity of football owes much
to the fact that it is one of the simplest sports in the world, with
only a handful of rules. Football can be played and enjoyed
anywhere by anyone from the slums of Mumbai to the beaches of
Brazil, from the schoolyards of Birmingham to the parking lots of
Johannesburg.

The premise of the this book

Football today attracts not only the athletically gifted. It has become the breeding ground for some of the best managers the world has ever seen. Due to the fact that professional football clubs have turnovers that would make most companies look small and insignificant, they need managers who can develop winning strategies, build winning teams, execute flawlessly and inspire millions of fans. These managers are not only ambitious and focused. In contrast to business managers, they are forced to be 100 percent results oriented, 24/7. The modern league system and the economic impact of the teams' results ensure an environment of hyper-competition. Very few professional managers can afford to lose more than a few matches. The results of being demoted to a lower league or not qualifying for a European tournament could be devastating and cost the club millions of pounds in lost revenue.

Hyper-competition means that football is a business like no other business. But at the same time football also encompasses some of the common aspects of all businesses: buying and selling assets, cost optimization, international relationships, finding and developing human resources, setting the team, developing winning strategies, goal-setting, etc. Football is a super-hostile competitive environment that ensures that only the strongest people and the best ideas survive. It is a formidable battlefield for learning and understanding management skills and issues. To quote Brady, Bolchover and Sturgess in their book, *The Talent Economy: The Football Model for Business*:

Football not only replicates the problems faced by business, but also intensifies them and accelerates the decision-making process by compressing the time-scale and heightening the focus owing to the relentless nature of media attention... Indeed, the very competitiveness of professional sport makes it not only a useful and entertaining model for business, but a necessary one. The very appeal of sports lies in its competitiveness – professional sport is the pinnacle of human competition. As competition in sport has intensified, we have witnessed a corresponding emphasis on the importance of the role of the manager. Football clubs needed managers almost as soon as players began to be paid openly after the Football Association legalized the practice in 1885.

The premise of this book is to analyse and learn from the managers of the best top professional football clubs. Since they have to perform in an environment of hyper-competition, they are faced with a relentless regime of management challenges, and an enormous pressure to deliver results. During our two years of research, interviews and testing it has been our goal to understand and define the ten most important traits of the top professional managers in Europe. We asked ourselves a number of simple questions such as:

- Why are they so good?
- What do they do?
- What do they say?
- How do they say it?
- What tools do they use?
- How do they implement?

Our empirical research concludes that the ten traits we have defined are more than relevant for today's business managers.

The challenge for business managers today is to find inspiration in the mastery of proven management tools. *Management by Football* provides exactly that. In order to give our readers the best possible opportunity to develop their own management skills, we have made available a "hands-on" management test that allows the business manager to compare his or her skills to the best professional football managers. The test is available at **www.managent-by-football.com**.

The national teams and the World Cup

Even though the main focus of *Management by Football* is the professional club manager, it cannot be denied that national football teams and their managers have become increasingly important over the last 30 years. In 2010 when the World Cup in South Africa takes place and the 24 best national teams meet, it will be the largest single sports and TV event in history. However, one must understand that the management challenges facing national team managers are very different from those facing their counterparts in the top European clubs.

For many years national teams did not get the respect, attention and funds they deserved. For the first 100 years of modern football, all the way through to the early 1980s, national football teams stood firmly in the shadow of the big professional clubs. The development of players, the recruitment of professional coaches, transfers, TV rights and so forth was primarily driven by the professional football clubs. Even though England appointed its first full-time manager in 1946, Walter Winterbottom, many smaller countries such as Denmark did not appoint full-time professional managers until the late 1970s. One of the main obstacles for changing the system was that the clubs owned the players and often denied them the opportunity to play for national teams.

However this was to change drastically throughout the 1970s and 1980s. There was a growing pressure from players and national football associations. Clubs realised that international tournaments such as the European Championship and the World Cup meant big business and a unique opportunity to showcase their most valuable assets, their players. This, combined with a drastically growing TV market, ensured that the formula for success was clear.

The large international tournaments for national football teams such as the European Championship and the World Cup have themselves become big institutions. During the 1998 World Cup in France an accumulated audience of more than 37 billion people followed the event on TV, while 1.3 billion followed the final alone (www.FIFA.com). The World Cup has also come to mean big business. During the 2006 World Cup in Germany, it is estimated that approximately 2 million tourists visited Germany during the month-long tournament. They spent an estimated 600 million Euros (www.dw-world.de). VISA is an official partner and sponsor of the

World Cup 2010 and 2014 and will pay $170 million for the privilege (June 27, 2007, Reuters). Adidas will extend its sponsorship agreement with FIFA to include the 2010 and 2014 World Cup, a mammoth deal worth $351 million (January 19, 2005, www.worldcup2010southafrica.com).

The top national team manager

National football associations have realised the importance of national teams as drivers and motivators for developing local talent both in terms of players and managers. There has also been increasing political pressure to ensure that national teams perform well. There is great prestige and marketing value in playing well for millions of people on TV. The marketing value of being exposed to markets around the world is enormous.

Today it is not uncommon to see top professional managers such as Fabio Capello, Marcello Lippi and Carlos Queiroz putting on national team jerseys. Out of the ten highest ranked teams going to the World Cup in South Africa, seven of the national team managers have had significant experience in major Europeans clubs and leagues. Six of them have won major national and international titles for their respective clubs, as shown in the following table:

1. Spain	Manager: Career: Achievements:	Vincente del Bosque Besiktas, Real Madrid, Real Madrid Castillas UEFA Champions League (2000, 2002), La Ligas (2001, 2003), Spanish Super Cup (2001), UEFA Euro, Super Cup (2002), Toyota Intercon. Cup (2002)
2. Brazil	Manager Career: Achievements:	Carlos Caetano Bledorn Verri (Dunga) - Copa America (2007), FIFA Confederations Cup (2009)
3. Netherlands	Manager Career: Achievements:	Bert van Marwijk Borussia Dortmund, Feyenoord, Fortuna Sittard, SV Meerssen, RKVCL Limmel, FC Herderen UEFA Cup (2002), Dutch Cup/KNVB Cup (2008)
4. Italy	Manager Career: Achievements:	Marcello Lippi Juventus, Internazionale, Napoli, Atalanta FIFA World Cup (2006), Interncon. Cup (1996), European Supercup (1996), Supercoppa Italiana (1995, 1997, 2002, 2003), Coppa Italia (1995), Serie A (1995, 1997, 1998, 2003)
5. Portugal	Manager Career: Achievements:	Carlos Queiroz Manchester United (Assistant), Real Madrid, South Africa, United Arab Emirates, Nagoya Grampus Eight, NY/NJ Metro Stars, Sporting CP, Portugal U-20 -
6. Portugal	Manager Career: Achievements:	Joachim Loew German National Team, Austria Wien, FC Tirol Innsbruck, Adanaspor, Karlsruher SC, Fenerbahche, VfB Stuttgart Euro 2008, Austrian Bundesliga (2002), DFB-Pokal (1997)
7. France	Manager Career: Achievements:	Ray Domenech France U-21, Lyon, Mulhouse -
8. Argentina	Manager Career: Achievements:	Diego Maradona Mandiyú de Corrientes, Racing -
9. England	Manager Career: Achievements:	Fabio Capello Real Madrid, Juventus, Roma, Milan La Liga (1997, 2007), Serie A (1992, 1993, 1994, 1996, 2001, 2005), UEFA Champions League (1995), European Super Cup (1994), Supercoppa Italianna (1992, 1993, 1994, 2001)
10. Cameroon	Manager Career: Achievements:	Paul Le Guen Paris Saint-Germain, Rangers, Olympique Lyonnais, Stade Rennais Ligue (2003, 2004, 2005), Trophée des Champions (2002, 2003, 2004), Coupe de la Ligue (2001, 2008)

(Source: www.fifa.com, www.wikipedia.com)

Only Brazil and Argentina have chosen to hire national managers with little management experience. Only Cameroon and England have opted to hire national managers with foreign nationalities. Most national football associations still believe strongly in hiring former local players or managers. However, it does not always give the best results.

Bringing in the top club managers to manage the national teams has also increased salaries significantly. The top paid national managers going to the World Cup 2010 all make more than £1.2 million, closing the gap to the club salaries. In 2009 the salaries of the top seven national managers and the top seven Premier League managers were reportedly as follows:

Rank	National Team Manager	Premier League Manager
1	Fabio Capello (England) £6,098.600	José Mourinho (Chelsea) £7,000,000
2	Marcello Lippi (Italy) £1,848,400	Arsene Wenger (Arsenal) £4,500,000
3	Bert van Marwijk (Netherlands) £1,663,600	Alex Ferguson (Man. United) £3,600,000
4	Otmar Hitzfeld (Switzerland) £1,602,000	David Moyes (Everton) £3,200,000
5	Joachim Loew (Germany) £1,417,500	Harry Redknapp (Tottenham) £3,000,000
6	Vicente Del Bosque (Spain) £1,355,800	Mark Hughes (Man. City) £3,000,000
7	Carlos Queiroz (Portugal) £1,232,700	Rafael Benitez (Liverpool0 £2,500,000

(Source: The Guardian 11.12.09, The Daily Dust, 5.3.09)

As the table illustrates **Fabio Capello** and **José Mourinho** were all in a class by themselves with mammoth salaries exceeding £6 million.

Mourinho has now taken this to a new level following his "triple" with Inter Milan (winning the League, the Copa Italia and the 2010 Champions League) with a move to Real Madrid for a package worth more than £10 million.

The Management Challenges of National Team Managers

The fundamental difference between club managers and national team managers are the number of games they each have an opportunity to play as well as the time they have available to practise with their respective teams. As **Bert van Marwijk**, national team manager for the Netherlands commented, it is a major challenge to build a meaningful working relationship with your players:

> *"An international coach has few opportunities to work with his squad. Because of that, I want to make the most of the time I spend with my players, mix with them, take part in training, and add and vary exercises, to get to know them better."*

National team managers have to be flexible in terms of practice, and try to fit it into the tide schedules of the professional clubs. Often players are tired from travelling, long club seasons or arrive late for training camps. These are all obstacles that increase the challenges of the national team manager.

The following table illustrates some of the main differences between club and national team managers:

	Club Manager (Premier League)	National Team Manager (England)
Games per season	• 38 league games • 0-30 tournament games (FA Cup, Champions League, European League, League Cup) • Training matches & Exhibition matches	• 11 games, 2009 season • 10 games, 2008 season
Training	• Long season • Many sessions	• Sporadic training • When opportunity is available
Ownership	• Owns the players	• Borrows the players
Team strategy	• Focus on core system and strategy for the team	• Must consider low frequency of training • Adopt players to system, or adopt system to players • Set plays are essential
Choice of players	• Budget restrictions, transfer windows, existing contracts	• Can choose between domestic and international players with the right passport
Contracts	• Players are tied to their club • Can be left out of the team, lent to other clubs or sold	• Players can be taken on and off the national team from one game to another
Criteria for success	• Long and continuous effort • A broad and strong team	• As much as 50 % of national games (in or out of tournament) are decided directly or indirectly by set plays.
Talent development	• Working closely together with scouts, second team and junior teams	• Working closely with their respective football associations to develop talent (U21/U17)

A national team manager has fewer games to prove himself. The low number of games increases the stakes for the manager and the team. It is a reality that a team's entry and access to the big championships such as the European Championship and the World Cup is determined by a few games. In contrast a premier league manager has 38 regular games in a season, lowering the stakes per game. However, today's national team manager has one great advantage over many club mangers, and that is that he has a whole nation's worth of players to pick and choose from, whereas club managers have to take into consideration their budget, the prevailing transfer windows, contracts signed by former managers and so forth.

One of the greatest challenges for any national team manager is to find the balance between (1) adopting a team strategy and requiring the players to fit in with it, or (2) building a strategy around the best players. The first option imposes a number of problems, as players are used to playing individual systems in their respective clubs. Furthermore, the low number of practice sessions does not facilitate building difficult team strategies. However it is also a challenge to build a system around the best players of a nation. Not only will they often be used to different playing systems, but the systems and the players might not be compatible. Either way, it is a challenge for the national manager to ensure that the team plays coherently and is able to achieve results.

The sporadic practice and low number of games played at national level may account for the fact that many national team games are won or lost by set plays. This is particularly true for tournament games such as The FIFA European Championship and FIFA World Cup. The consequence is that many national managers spend considerable time understanding opponent's strategies for set plays as well developing and training their own set plays. Set plays are easier to remember and practise for teams that have less practice time together.

Many national team managers have an important role together with their respective national football associations to develop and nurture talents – as in the case of **Morten Olsen**, manager of the

Danish national team going to South Africa. He has played a vital part in setting up a strategy for developing talented players in Denmark. Together with the Danish Football Association (DBU), he has been one of the driving forces in shaping the training programmes at boys', youths' and senior level.

Lastly, it is essential that the national team manager is able to not only to qualify for the big tournaments but also to rally a nation as they enter an international tournament. The manager is seen by the millions of national and international fans as the nation's representative – the face it presents to the world. This is one of the reasons that many countries prefer to hire high-profile ex-players from their national leagues, who already have a strong reputation and following, although this may not always create the best results. It is interesting to note that **Fabio Capello** is only the second foreigner to take charge of the English national team.

From a management point of view, the national team manager's job has similar characteristics to those of a business manager working in an organisation with a project-based structure. The manager has only limited access to the team, and team members might have very different tasks on other teams. The manager borrows or rents team players from other departments, and the players have other managers they have to answer to for other projects.

The World Cup, England and Fabio Capello

It is very true that the English national team has a special place in the hearts of fans, not only in England, but around the globe. An international tournament, such as the European Championship or the World Cup, is not the same without England. England is the birthplace of modern football and every time an English team participates in an international tournament the pressure to win and perform is tremendous. In a sense England is the keeper and owner of the true football culture and has influenced how the world perceives and understands football.

Since England's last World Cup triumph in 1966, England has been more than eager to repeat the success. The development of the English national team over the last three years indicates that England have a very potent national team and might have a real shot at the World Cup title. Not only does England have the strongest league in the world, The Premier League, it has also fostered some of the biggest all time football players and managers. This is a league where the best players and managers from around the world are more than eager to compete. Many of the key players from the national team such as Wayne Rooney, Rio Ferdinand and John Terry are at the heights of their careers. Add to this formula one of the best managers in the world, **Fabio Capello**.

To illustrate that England and the FA mean business, Fabio Capello was signed up as the English national team manager in December 2007, closing one of the largest manager contracts the world has ever seen. Fabio Capello has won everything there is to win as a club manager, and it did not take long for him to do his magic with the English national team. From the very start there has been a talk about the "Capello effect" and his impact on the team.

At the time of writing this book, the English national team is rated number 9 in the world. A history of the England team's rankings under recent managers is illustrated below:

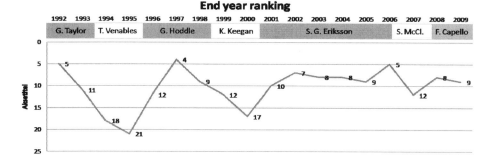

(Source: www.fifa.com)

Even though the current FIFA ranking as number 9 is four places below the number 5 rating achieved by **Sven Goran Eriksson**, it is apparent to everyone that the team is undergoing a tremendous change for the better. Under Fabio Capello England has won all but one of the qualifying games for the World Cup 2010. A 5-1 victory over Croatia at Wembley Stadium ensured that the qualification was a reality and with no less than two games to spare.

There is no doubt that Fabio Capello is a manager from the school of discipline. He demands respect and radiates authority. He is a pragmatist, a master strategist and tactician who is 100 percent focused on winning – all the time. Everything he does has that one purpose. This attitude influences every choice he makes as a manager that being everything from the choice of hotel to the table manners of the team. As a matter of fact, Fabio Capello has set down ground rules for the team. Simple but important rules. For example, he has stated that suits are to be worn to and from matches, mobile phones are to be switched off during meal times and meetings, meetings are to be attended promptly, no visitors at the team hotel, no nick-names, only use of surnames, etc. (*source: A. Ananth, Goal.com UK, 11.12.09*). Fabio Capello put it this way in his own words:

> *"I don't accept lack of respect. That means be on time, respect the dressing-room code and table manners. They are necessary rules to create a group. Functioning in this manner at clubs that I managed has always given results...So I apply the same in the England national Team."*
>
> (The Sun, 11.12.09)

However, the most important challenge for Fabio Capello has been to invigorate and reignite the self-esteem and the will to win. When Fabio Capello took charge in December 2007, he inherited a team that had failed to qualify for the European Championship in 2008, with players who seemed afraid to play and completely lacking in self-belief. Self-esteem and the will to win are essential for top football teams. The players from the top national teams around the world are all world class. Their technical skills are superb; they are in great condition. As so often quoted in the world of sports, the difference between the number one and the number two is merely a state of mind.

What Fabio Capello has done for the English national Team can be summed up in a very few words. In short, he has prescribed a line of tough discipline, with set rituals all with the aim of building self-esteem and the will to win. Together with his superb sense of strategy and tactics, he has quickly built a self-energising momentum of winning, and has assembled what is undoubtedly one of the strongest English teams ever going into a World Cup tournament.

However, we will need to wait for the final whistle of the World Cup 2010 before we find out if the unique talents and ingenuity of Capello, Rooney & Co. are enough to bring home the biggest trophy on the planet. What is certain is that if England *are* successful, there are many people around the world, of all nationalities, who would happily applaud the return of the trophy to the country that fostered the greatest sport and business on earth.

THE BUSINESS OF FOOTBALL

You arrive at work as usual, well aware that:

- Your work is being reviewed and commented on by millions.
- Many of your employees earn more than you do.
- Even if you deliver results, there is no guarantee how long you will keep your job.
- Your best employees leave your company several times a year to work for someone else. You still pay their wages and risk having them come back without them being able to perform their duties.
- You are a public person. Everything you do and say is broadcast via television and online to the entire world.
- Your employees are a mix of people from a wide range of different nationalities and cultures.
- You must deliver outstanding results every time!

Not many people would want such a job. Nevertheless, this is pretty much the job that Fabio Capello, Arsene Wenger, Sir Alex Ferguson, José Mourinho, Rafael Benitez and a number of other men have. They are managers of some of the world's best football teams. Every tiny detail they are in charge of is evaluated by millions of spectators, the world press, powerful club shareholders and their thousands (or hundreds of thousands) of "hardcore fans".

Most people will agree with us that the above sounds like an unusual job. But the tasks that football's top managers handle are very similar to the challenges we face as managers in both private and public sectors – except that they work under much tougher conditions! Therefore we can all become better leaders by studying, and learning from, these men.

Why did we write this book?

"The spirit of an organisation is created from the top," the king of management gurus, Peter Drucker, has been quoted as saying. The quote summarises exactly what management is about, and why the manager's role can never be underestimated. Every unit/division/company is centred on him/her, and he/she is responsible for reaching the goals outlined.

There are as many definitions of management as there are managers. One simple definition is that management is about getting other people to do something. A more detailed definition comes from Professor Erik Johnsen (econ. dr., dr.h.c. at Copenhagen Business School), who writes that management can be defined by the following characteristics: "a communicating interaction between people, which enables the sharing of knowledge and physical resources in order to provide a practical solution so that a specified goal can be reached."[1]

In short, we perceive management as the process you have to go through in order to achieve results. The difference between good and bad management can, literally, be measured by any company's results. Good management makes us utilise our resources to the utmost and ensures that we reach the goals we have set out. But is good management always being practised? No, sadly this is not the case. In an analysis by the Copenhagen Business School and Stig Jørgensen & Partners of the relationship between quality of management and profitability, the following is among the conclusions:

It turns out that we apparently have a problem with poor management throughout the business sector. A large survey based on a sample of 2,000 managers from the 'European Employee Index' database shows that one in two managers is skilled academically, but lacks the leadership needed to motivate and engage employees, and one in ten managers are so poor that, according to the employees, they need extensive support in the form of education, training and coaching – or perhaps should not be managers at all. According to the survey, only one quarter of managers qualify to be called "complete", meaning that both their academic and managerial qualifications are adequate.

Another survey, carried out by consultancy Cubiks, shows that if employees encounter bad management, in two out of three instances it may lead them to leave the company. Today, employees have high expectations of the manager both on a professional and a personal level. The manager must show enthusiasm, insight and faith in the employee. The survey also finds that 87 percent of Danes have not done their best at work because of bad managers. This percentage is so high that no other country in the survey comes close to it.[2]

But what has gone wrong? Why is there a lot of good management, but even more not-so-good management? There is no shortage of literature offering guidance on improved management techniques, and every manager has his own library of books providing recipes for high-performance teams, efficient tactics for reaching goals, remuneration models, motivational factors and so on. In other words, a lack of ideas is not the problem.

Football – the source of inspiration

The challenge lies more in building a bridge between what is good management and the world we as managers live in. Far too often we read books and attend courses about the latest trends in management. And far too often we forget or do not get the point because it is too far away from our everyday life.

That is exactly why football is the exception as a learning tool. Football is the world's most watched and played sport. And we all have clear memories of experiences from this universe. Most Danes, for example, remember Euro '92 (the first major tournament they ever won). In the same way, any Manchester United fan remembers the club's amazing comeback against Bayern Munich in the Champions League final of 1999. Using football to put management into perspective makes it easier for us to remember the good examples and learn from the men who practise management at its highest level.

Futurologist Rolf Jensen wrote the following in the book *Heartstorm*:

> *The professional sports club's supporters are loyal buyers of the club's "brand". Often, they even buy into it when the team is performing poorly. This is an interesting case of brand loyalty, which – if it could be transferred to the branded goods market – would result in the consumer sticking to his brand, even though he knew other brands were better.*[3]

What Rolf Jensen writes, any football fan already knows: football fans will follow their team through good and bad. We do that because football is a game of emotions. We live, to various degrees, for our clubs. So we remember things that have happened on the field much more clearly and for longer than things we read and hear about in other places. Therefore, lessons from the world of football are remembered better and more clearly than things taken from an article, a book or a course with traditional management as the focal point. By using football as the point of departure, our goal is to motivate and engage you as a reader in a more powerful way than you are by a "normal" book about management.

The football manager is the natural focal point of this book as he chooses the team, decides the playing style, tactics and so on – in each case a task similar to yours as a manager.

Anyone who doubts the relevance of football management as a general business model might ask themselves two questions:

1) To what extent is the top football manager's tasks similar to that of the "normal" manager?
2) Why might football managers be better managers than I am?

The short answers are: 1) To a very large extent. 2) Because they work under even more pressure than top business leaders. If you want more in-depth argumentation, please read the next chapter.

The world of football vs. the world of business

A company's most important resource will always be the people working for it. A unique product rarely remains unique for a long time. A favourable market position can quickly be undermined and taken over by your worst competitor. And you will always meet someone willing to sell a product similar to yours at a cheaper price. But surrounded by the right team of people, you are in a position to respond to the competition's move and create a winning counter strike.

To manage a group of people is an important mission, and the way in which the management of people is executed has an influence on the company's results, as well as being of great importance to the employees. In this respect, this is the most important issue within a company.

The same goes for the world of football. The way in which a leading football manager acts has influence on the players, the club, shareholders, fans and sometimes the mood of an entire nation. For example, just take a look at Brazil during a World Cup or Copa de America final, or Germany's re-emergence during the 2006 World Cup.

The leading international football managers practise management in a world of many different stakeholders, all of whom have enormous expectations. Not only do they have to bring home local and international trophies every year. The trophies have to be won in style, too!

During the 2005/2006 season, **Fabio Capello** was manager for Real Madrid. He was expected to win at least the national league. During the latter half of the season he was surrounded by die-hard rumours that Real Madrid's president, Ramon Calderon, wanted a new manager. Capello did successfully guide Real Madrid to the Spanish championship – and was fired two weeks later. The way in which he won was simply not entertaining enough for Real Madrid's many supporters and shareholders. As Bernd Schuster put it shortly after taking up the job of new manager: "You don't just have to win titles, you have to make sure you entertain the supporters while you're doing it."[4]

José Mourinho was in the same situation while Chelsea manager: "At one point during last season, 14 different managers were rumoured to be after my job. Had I not had a strong mentality at that time, I would probably have bowed to pressure and left."[5]

It was not enough to provide great results. They must be second to none. Chelsea chief executive Peter Kenyon has revealed that team owner **Roman Abramovich** has a ten-year plan for the club, among other things stating that the club must win the Champions League twice during that time. Kenyon added: "It's about winning in a style – in a matter – befitting one of the best clubs in Europe."[6]

A top football manager's world is, thus, tough, and only the best survive. They must act in a world full of powerful stakeholders who have one clear demand: Victory, every single time!

And the budgets in the world of football are by no means small. An analysis by international accounting firm Deloitte shows that the combined revenue of the top 20 clubs in Europe was £3 billion in 2007/08 (source: Deloitte: Lost in translation. Football Money League). European football had revenue equivalent to £9 billion in 2006.

Let us take a look at the kind of sums the world of football operates with:

Premier League's presumably most expensive buys during summer break 2007

Player	Amount (£m)	Clubs
Fernando Torres	26	from Atletico Madrid to Liverpool
Anderson	18	from FC Porto to Manchester United
Owen Hargreaves	17	from Bayern Munich to Manchester United
Nani	17	from Sporting to Manchester United
Darren Bent	17	from Charlton to Tottenham

Florent Malouda	14	from Lyon to Chelsea
Ryan Babel	12	from Ajax to Liverpool
Craig Gordon	9	from Hearts to Sunderland
Rolando Binachi	9	from Reggina to Manchester City
Eduardo da Silva	8	from Dinamo Zagreb to Arsenal

Source: "Premier League's most expensive buys" www.eb.dk 10 August 2007.

Top 10 Overall Transfers

1. Cristiano Ronaldo: Manchester United to Real Madrid – £80m (2009)
2. Kaka: AC Milan to Real Madrid – £56m (2009)
3. Zinedine Zidane: Juventus to Real Madrid – £45.62m (2001)
4. Luis Figo: Barcelona to Real Madrid – £37m (2000)
5. Hernan Crespo: Parma to Lazio – £35.5m (2000)
6. Gianluigi Buffon: Parma to Juventus – £32.6m (2001)
7. Robinho: Real Madrid to Manchester City – £32.5m (2008)
8. Christian Vieri: Lazio to Inter – £32m (1999)
9. Dimitar Berbatov: Tottenham to Manchester United – £30.75m (2008)
10. Andriy Shevchenko: AC Milan to Chelsea – £30m (2006)

Source: http://soccerlens.com/top-10-most-expensive-transfers-in-football/5244/

The above figures illustrate that top football managers make decisions that are at least as significant as those of leading business managers. We are talking *large* sums that these managers have discretion to spend. These amounts of money put increased pressure on their performance, making it especially important that they achieve great results – not only in their own national leagues, but also on a European level.

Deloitte partner Jesper Jørgensen is the Danish contributor to Deloitte's regular report on European football. He says it is difficult to overstate the value of the football manager:

*"Managers such as **Mourinho**, **Ferguson** and **Laudrup** have a charismatic personality that gives the clubs they manage priceless amounts of brand value. This attracts even more spectators, increased TV coverage, a larger pool of sponsors and so on. For example, **José Mourinho** has played a very important role creating Chelsea's brand. Try comparing the news headlines he has generated to those of **Avram Grant**. Then you know just how important charismatic top manager are."[7]*

FC Barcelona vice president Ferran Soriano told Børsen Executive Club that his main philosophy is that the club should be run just like any other kind of business. And he has had considerable success in following this line. The club went from posting major losses to becoming profitable, and this has helped get rid of large parts of debts that have burdened the club for many years.[8]

Rakesh Sondhi, international strategy and management consultant and MBA lecturer at Henley Management College says it even more directly:

"I think there is a considerable amount that the business manager can learn from the football manager. The football manager has to deliver results that are very tangible. In many companies, the results are too far away from many teams as the performance criteria have not been cascaded down effectively. The football manager has to perform in an environment where the pressure is intense and outcomes of non-delivery are clinical, i.e. there is the sack."[9]

Why is the world of football a good source of inspiration and role models? The conclusion is clear: top football managers operate in a world that in many ways is similar to that of any other manager. Only multiply that by 100!

There is no big difference between the responsibilities of a football manager and a business leader

The football manager's responsibilities	The business leader's responsibilities
Create the perfect football team	Create the perfect unit, executive group, etc.
Buy and sell players	Hire and fire employees
Set out goals for the tournament	Set out goals for the division, the company, etc.
Decide the playing system	Decide the strategy
Coach and develop the players	Coach and develop the players
Ensure good relations with the press	Ensure good relations with the press
Make sure shareholders are happy	Make sure shareholders are happy
Control individualists and team players	Control individualists and team players
Motivate the team	Motivate the team
Secure and execute an optimal budget	Secure and execute and optimal budget
Et cetera	Et cetera

Does this sound like *your* job as a manager? Probably! Besides this, as stated earlier, the top football manager has to operate in a world of many different, powerful stakeholders. Just have a look at the following model:

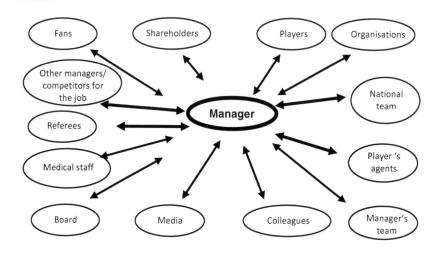

The model shows – in football terms – a score-draw of 1-1 between the football world and the world in which other top managers operate! Unlike football managers, however, other managers have the advantage that their work is not being evaluated on every match day! Almost all companies are judged by quarterly results, press releases about new initiatives, senior managers' appearance in the press and so on. This takes place from time to time during a calendar year. To a top football manager, the situation is somewhat different. Their work is sometimes judged several times a week, directly via broadcast television, and gets evaluated through countless written words in print and online media.

Add to this that his work is carried out under the influence of a certain amount of *chance*. "Football is the centre of injustice," said Danish national team manager **Morten Olsen**.[10] As an example, leading Danish team FC Copenhagen managed to qualify to the Champions League for the first time with the help of, among other things, a home goal by Dutch side Ajax Amsterdam.

At the same time, the football manager (like you, probably) has to accept that he can't go onto the pitch and create the results himself. Like you, he has to work through people, and thereby make sure that the organisation's strategy is implemented and the desired objectives are reached.

The manager is, like the business leader, the coach who has to make the team function. No matter if we are talking about a large multinational conglomerate, a local industrial company, a marketing department or a shop, it is the manager's responsibility to make things work and reach the organisation's goals.

The leading football managers know how to deliver. During our research for this book, we asked several sources who their role models are. One of the managers most often mentioned is Arsenal's **Arsene Wenger.**

Throughout his career in the club, he has won England's Premier League three times, the FA Cup four times and the Charity/Community Shield four times. His coaching and eye for talent is unique. He moved Thierry Henry from a wing position to become one of the best strikers in the world. He was also among the first managers to employ a dietician who could tell what the players needed in order to be in best possible shape. It was also Wenger who made all major decisions in connection with the development of Arsenal's revolutionary training facility.

When Wenger approved the sale of Henry to Barcelona, many fans and football writers seriously questioned his decision. Having scored 224 goals for Arsenal, Henry was the club's best-scoring player ever. But it turned out that Wenger once again had a gift for spotting rising stars ready to take over. As he said: "We're trying to compensate for that with the blossoming of our young players, by greater use of initiative, by sharing responsibility at the heart of the side which was sometimes a bit too concentrated on one player from an attacking point of view."[11]

A unique person among football managers, he has also been named FA Premier League Manager of the Year three times.

What to expect from the book

This is not a traditional book about management. It contains no "heavy" analysis. It does not approach the topic from a deep, theoretical perspective. What it does give you is an example of how *others* practise good management. Anyone with a management role in the private, public and non-commercial sectors can find inspiration in this study, and can learn important lessons from the world of football management which will enable them to become better managers in their own worlds.

Each chapter is structured in the same way:

1) An example from the world of football relating to the chapter's topic.
2) Putting the relationship with the business world into perspective.

By doing this, it is our goal that you, as a reader, will find it easy to remember the book's main points and will find inspiration to make a positive difference in your capacity as a manager. At www.management-by-football.com you can also test your competences.

How we did it

In order to find out what has already been written on the subject, we have read more than 10,000 pages of books about and by the best international football managers. We have dug into so many local and international newspapers, magazines, TV reports and online articles that we have stopped counting (we are talking hundreds of articles and many, many hours of TV interviews and reports). Finally, we have interviewed top football managers and players. Not only in order to get to the source, but also to hear how their management is perceived by the players. Furthermore, we have interviewed sports journalists specialising in football, as they often have access to information unavailable to others.

We have taken particular interest in top managers in England, Spain, Italy, Germany and France. These countries have the biggest economic power, the most spectators and fans, and have won 75 percent of all Champions League titles.

We could have chosen to focus on some of the many excellent national team managers in charge of some of the world's best football sides. But their management duties are largely different from those of club managers. In particular, they are only responsible for the players for a short period of time during the year, and they can only select players from one country.

What to learn from the world of football

After a long process of thoroughly studying football's best managers, we have come up with a list of 10 of their competencies that we believe we can learn a lot from. The list is by no means exhaustive, and every single point could justify a book on its own. But each and every competence makes a difference! Learn from them and you will become an even better manager.

- The first competence: Go for gold.
- The second competence: Explain "why".
- The third competence: Turn strategy into behaviour.
- The fourth competence: Make your strategy flexible.
- The fifth competence: Find the right people.
- The sixth competence: Develop the second tier talent.
- The seventh competence: Create good coaching habits.
- The eighth competence: Empower problem-solvers.
- The ninth competence: Know your competitor.
- The tenth competence: Exploit set-piece situations.

THE FIRST COMPETENCE
GO FOR GOLD

On 20 September 1995, Manchester United played host to Division Two side York City in the second round of the Coca-Cola Cup. As the day came to a close, one of modern football's biggest upsets was a reality. York City had beaten Manchester United's stars 3-0. A fortnight later, the surprise was complete when Manchester United only managed to win 3-1 in the return match in York. York City manager **Alan Little** had achieved the impossible. Manchester United were out of the tournament. The team had used all its superstars over the two legs – Peter Schmeichel, Ryan Giggs, David Beckham, Paul Scholes, Eric Cantona and others – but it hadn't helped.

Almost as surprising was the result when **Otto Rehhagel** made Greece European champions in 2004. Greece, a relatively insignificant football nation, came from nowhere to beat the best and take the European cup. Before the 2004 tournament, Greece had never even won a match in a European final tournament.

What can we learn from these exceptional football achievements?

Football managers always go for gold

One thing almost all managers and football players have in common is the belief that they have a chance of winning the next match, no matter who the other side is. As managers and players they have grown up with a "go for gold" mentality. It is almost blasphemy to set foot on the football pitch without giving your utmost and trying to win the match, no matter who you are playing against.

The football manager's destiny is to "go for gold", no matter how strong the opponent is, how exhausted his team is and how many of his players are injured. Losing is not an option.

What does "go for gold" mean?

Business leaders can learn a lot from professional football managers and their "go for gold" approach. The immediate conclusion is that we, as business leaders, must be much better at believing we will win every time, no matter what obstacle or challenge we face.

Most professional football managers are not only good at believing they must "go for gold"! They are also brilliant at motivating and convincing their players to do the same. Prior to the kickoff of the 2003/2004 season, Arsenal manager **Arsene Wenger** proclaimed he would go through the season without losing a single match. Most fans and journalists were quite sceptical. But Wenger had planted a seed of hope in his players' minds, and Arsenal finished the season without any defeats in the Premier League.

Football is about winning every match. Judging a manager and his team is painfully easy. Did the team win the latest match? Did the team win the national league? Did the team qualify for the next final round?

In the world of business, things are much more complicated. As business leaders, we have a much harder time identifying and defining clear objectives, and it is even more difficult to evaluate accomplishments. From time to time, you will come across companies and business leaders who deliberately avoid setting out clear targets in order to avoid being judged on their achievement (or non-achievement). They simply do not want to expose their weak results.

Football's clear and focused evaluation of teams is central to the "go for gold" approach. Most managers and football players have turned their hobby into work. They are very passionate about football and are personally extremely motivated. Since many of us have joined the world of business out of necessity rather than passion, we often do not have the same sense of commitment or willingness to sacrifice whatever it takes. We have all met business leaders who have turned down good projects because it would take an extra effort. All this makes it much harder to identify the right objectives, the right presentation and to separate winners from losers.

One of the most ambitious attempts at putting employee performance at the centre took place at GE. Jack Welch introduced the rule that all managers every year should evaluate every single employee and fire the bottom 10%. The idea was that, over a period of 10 to 15 years, GE would create one of the best work forces in the world.[12] GE's results – continued growth throughout the years – and the fact that today it is one of the world's most respected companies speak for themselves.

We love football

Throughout the years there has been written a lot about why football is the world's most popular sport, and why it has turned into such a huge industry. We believe there are three simple reasons why football has become so popular.

First of all, most of us have known football from when we were very young. We have literally been fed football via nursery school, primary school, the media and the clubs. Even those who did not play as youngsters have been influenced so much that they have a good knowledge of the world of football before they leave school.

Secondly, the simplicity of the game means that anyone can play football anywhere. It does not require much more than a few square metres and something that resembles a football. Leave the rest to the imagination. This goes whether we are talking about the ghettos of large Asian cities, Brazil's beaches or small villages in Africa. Football is so simple that in reality it has no more than a handful of rules.

Thirdly, football engages people. It brings the best and worst out in us. Football can lead to great physical and emotional accomplishments, but can also generate violence and crime. The game is, in its simplicity, brutally honest, and there is rarely any doubt about which team you support, or who won and who lost. The strong sense of competition makes people emotional. Whenever there is a World Cup or UEFA Cup final, millions of people around the world follow it. Over the last 50 years, we have countless times witnessed entire cities or populations becoming ecstatic following international victories.

As managers, players and fans of football, we are deeply emotionally involved in the sport. In the world of business that is more the exception than the rule. As managers we should ask ourselves if we are satisfied with this exception. We are convinced that most companies that take this type of commitment and winning mentality seriously can create the same results.

Characteristics of a professional football manager
We are convinced that professional football managers who always "go for gold" have four important characteristics. They are:

- Courage and will
- The ability to look beyond the immediate
- A strong personal passion for their work
- Willingness to sacrifice

Courage and will
A great football manager and leader must have the personality and willingness to take risks. You cannot win championships and tournaments if you lose or draw all the time.

A great football manager knows he has to gamble in order to win, because the competition from the other teams is very intense. Many matches are decided by small factors. Will the shot hitting the crossbar become a goal or not? Will the team be awarded a penalty shot or will the referee let the game go on?

Speaking in business terms, this means that we as business leaders should be much better at challenging and believing that we can make a difference all the time. We must train ourselves to believe that "being happy with a draw" or a "small defeat" is never the best option. As leaders, we should begin and end the "season" by believing we can win – and win every single match. As with Alan Little of York City we must dare to challenge the impossible and expect to beat Manchester United at their home ground. If we believe in this, we have given ourselves the chance of obtaining success and outstanding performances.

In football – and also in business – you cannot win matches by thinking mediocre results are acceptable, and that everything else will be fine. It is impossible to win a tournament if all your matches end in a draw.

As Apple's Steve Jobs once noted, we must dare to put a ding in the universe, or we might as well stay at home.

Honestly, in our business careers have we not all at least once felt the lack of courage and character to challenge? Be it a boss, a project or a supplier. In the world of business, we have got used to political games, workplace tactics and hidden agendas that infiltrate our companies and help disrupt our goals and performances. It is tempting to ask when your company last time entered the field as a team well aware that you share a common faith – and that losing is not an option.

These are the conditions that many professional football managers in clubs such as Scotland's Celtic, Barcelona, Real Madrid and AC Milan work under. The manager, players and fans all expect to win every single match. The manager faces enormous pressure, and many supporters do not accept when their team loses.

Often in the world of business, people believe performances are created by individuals rather than groups. Many people think that the best chance of survival for their company is to take no chances, play it safe and never challenge the status quo. This is an extremely dangerous illusion for business leaders, because behaviour like this leads to indifference and the simple fact is that these companies slowly will get caught up, swallowed by competitors and abandoned by their customers who have found better products and services elsewhere.

Without doubt companies such as Apple, Google, Starbucks and Dell have had the courage to challenge the status quo. Often have we seen, for example, Apple challenge the mighty Microsoft and challenge the way consumers perceive the company's products. Google challenged market leader Yahoo! without even having a business model, solely driven by the belief in, and will to, develop the world's best search engine.[13] Starbucks challenged consumers and the way in which we drank coffee. And Dell challenged giant IBM and the way we build and sell computers.

Some might argue that many companies have failed going down the path of Apple, Google and Dell. That may very well be true. But all those companies that had the guts, but did not make it and never became famous, actually created something huge. Something very important. They helped create new products, new ways to look at consumer behaviour, new production methods and much more. They have been a "stepping stone" for the *successful* companies and a constant source of inspiration to keep the old guard of companies alert.

The late Leo Burnett, who together with Bernbach and Ogilvy was the man behind modern advertising, put it this way: "When you reach for the stars, you may not quite get one, but you won't come up with a handful of mud either."[14]

The ability to look beyond the immediate

A great football manager and leader will have the ability and intuition to look beyond the status quo. As a manager and leader you have to be able to look at your team not only from a tactical perspective, but also from a strategic perspective. When it comes to the tactical perspective, the leader knows that success will be measured by the latest match – did he win or not? Nonetheless, it is evident that the football manager can set future targets without knowing how to reach them when time comes. This takes quite a lot of courage.

Objectives have to be challenging for the team even if the manager at that point might have doubts about how to reach them. He simply must motivate and engage his team. To set out objectives that are greater than the team's present performance ensures that the team and its competences are challenged continuously. It is an outstanding tool to make sure your team or company stays ahead of the competition.

As an example, during the late 90s Chelsea set out a target to become European champions twice in a decade and at the same time dominate the Premier League.[15]

The club has not yet reached its target, but it has triggered a furious development. And one of the results is that the club became English champions back-to-back in 2005 and 2006.

Our experience tells us that too many companies claim to have strategic and motivating objectives. These objectives may indeed be of a strategic nature, but they are not worth fighting for and will not help you beat the competition. Increasing sales by 25 percent is not a motivating and developing objective. This is a direct path to indifference and leads to the risk of ending up the same as the manufacturers of the typewriter, horse carriage and stencil. A slow, but certain death.

We need to set out objectives that trigger development, knowledge and innovation. Objectives that can help engage, motivate and support employees in their daily work. It is not satisfying to be efficient and win the "battle" if you lose the "war" in the end.

One of the most famous examples of the ability to look beyond the immediate belongs to late US President John F. Kennedy. In the early 60s, he set out the goal that America would have a man on the Moon and back again by the end of the decade. Scientists and engineers were terrified by this "impossible" project. Computer technology was in its infancy, civil aviation had only just begun, and launching rockets with satellites into space was basically playing Russian roulette. Often, they would burn up on the launch ramp or explode and turn into huge fireballs. But Kennedy knew what was coming. The Cold War and fear of the Russians were an incredible inspiration to Americans. Hundreds of science projects were initiated, and they created a continuous flow of thousands of innovations that would later be used by thousands of companies worldwide.

Winning the "space race" ahead of the Russians was an objective worth fighting for to the Americans, and it motivated thousands of people. The alternative was simply not an option.

The ability to look beyond the immediate brings with it the duty to make decisions. As business leaders, you often have to make decisions that are highly unpleasant or unpopular. In his book *A Will to Win*, Manchester United manager **Sir Alex Ferguson**[16] writes that in May 1996 he felt he had to get rid of very well-regarded players Mark Hughes, Paul Ince and Andrei Kanchelskis. Ferguson was convinced that during the next few seasons the team needed to build new competences in order to reach the top. His decision was not very popular among experts and fans. But Sir Alex knew what was coming and turned the club into one of the most winning in history. In the following years, Manchester United won the English premiership six times, the Champions League twice and the FA Cup and League Cup once each.

A strong personal passion for their work

One of the greatest advantages of football is passion. All the famous football managers throughout time have had a real passion for the sport. People such as Hennes Weisweiler, Udo Latek, Helenio Herrera, José Mourinho, Juande Ramos and many more live for football. Their many championships and huge performances are a testimony to this.

Many great football managers have had a passion for football from a very young age and turned their hobby and talent into a job in itself. Often, they are former professional players themselves. We rarely see this kind of "luxury" in the world of business. In many cases, we are not that interested in business until we reach our 20s and have to choose a further education. And often it is the result of us not being able to fulfil other dreams. We all know the kind of leaders that are leaders simply in order to get the next pay cheque. They have no calling and no passion. To them, the status quo and no challenges are the most important things in the world. In the world of business, it is hard to find managers who see management as their top priority.

In our experience, when the match is over and the points have been divided, passion comes out as the winner. A manager passionate about football and his team is willing to use every resource available down to the last penny to make his team as good as possible. Courage, will and the ability to look beyond the immediate – combined with a burning passion – will motivate your assistant managers and players. And they know that you will do everything you can to reach your goals.

Within the venture capital industry, investors are looking for more than simply raw talent and a strong business plan. Many investors know from experience that it is often more important to have a real passion for what you do. People who love what they do will spend all their money and time on it. Passion beats everything else.

As Apple's Steve Jobs said during a graduation ceremony at Stanford in 2005, the most important thing is to find "the" thing that you love. When you find it, you are capable of creating outstanding results. Even if you have to start out in a garage with no money at all.

Willingness to sacrifice

Sacrifice is a core component of the "go for gold" mentality. As a manager, you have to be ready to sacrifice what is needed in order to create great results.

Because of the tough competition and transparency in the construction of the football league system, there is an immense rivalry between teams and managers. It is very difficult to become manager of a large club without having made sacrifices on the way. Sacrifices necessary in order to have a shot at becoming a professional manager. In *A Will to Win*, **Sir Alex Ferguson**[17] several times describes how an average day is full of training, meetings, charity events, travels, interviews and much more. Not many moments are left to share with family and friends. And spare time is minimal.

Passion and the willingness to sacrifice go hand in hand. Obviously, a great football manager has to make sacrifices in other areas to make room for football. As a professional manager has a very busy day with many tasks and lots of travel, it is inevitable that his family, friends and spare time will suffer. Countless hours are spent training with the team, and in the evenings there are match videos to watch and match fixtures to plan.

Perhaps less obvious is the fact that there are also sacrifices to be made *within* the world of football. Often, a manager has to sacrifice personal relations with players, assistant managers and maybe other managers as his career develops. It is lonely at the top, and you cannot be friends with everyone. Professional relations can change without notice if an assistant manager suddenly becomes your competitor, or a key player joins your arch rivals.

Opposing teams are not the only threat to a manager. In many cases, success will kill the passion and willingness to sacrifice and take chances. Success can create a feeling of having reached your objective and now it is time to maintain it without taking too many risks. The conclusion from this process is wrong from a competitive perspective. Successful managers sometimes forget that what made them successful is the same thing that is needed to achieve success in the future. It is the same recipe.

In our experience, somewhere out there, there is someone willing to work even harder than you. Someone willing to sacrifice even more. Someone who has the passion, courage and will to challenge the status quo. Someone who will develop a product or service far better than yours. That is why a good manager never relaxes and never accepts second best. You cannot take out insurance against two guys in a garage or a college student who does not care about profit or business plans. These people are willing to sacrifice more than you. Yahoo! learned this from Google. IBM learned it from Dell. Passion wins.

Conclusion

There are a number of important points that we as business leaders can learn from the "go for gold" mentality. The extremely fierce competition within professional football has created several outstanding leaders with unique competences.

As a business leader, the following key points will be useful to you.

- "Always go for gold" no matter what the challenge or competition.
- Build up courage and the will to gamble.
- Challenge the status quo and set out new objectives, even if you may not have the solution.
- Always look beyond the immediate situation.
- Unpopular decisions may lead to new successes.
- Have a passion for your work.
- Be willing to sacrifice what it takes to win every time.

To "go for gold" is not a trend or a sudden thought. To "go for gold" is equally important whether you have just started out your career or have reached the top already. The best managers "go for gold" every day and every time.

Find courage and will. Dive in today and "go for gold".

THE SECOND COMPETENCE
EXPLAIN "WHY"

There is never any doubt when we see a football team with a well-founded strategy. For instance an Inter team under the leadership **José Mourinho** that changes between world class defence and quick powerplay. Or it could be FC Barcelona with **Josep Guardiola** in front totally dominating a match using world-class midfield players and passing. We have also witnessed it when Chelsea and **Carlo Ancelotti** destroy the opponents' defence with a mix of world class passes and attacking ingenuity.

But what does it take to implement a strategy in a team that each season takes part in 3-4 different national and international tournaments? A team that faces local premiership competitors as well as international top sides. A team that has to cope with both success and failure, buying and selling players, injuries and matches with several men down.

Change creates victories

Mourinho, Guardiola and Ancelotti all know that a well-founded strategy is the way to a lot of victories. It is no coincidence that a team with a well-founded strategy makes the play look easy. The players know where their colleagues are standing and running and anticipate all the competitors' next moves.

But to found a strategy requires a lot of planning, preparation and not least a deep understanding of how to turn strategy into concrete action on the ground.

In business, as in football, no matter what strategy you choose to pursue, there are three fundamental elements you have to get right to achieve success:

- System
- Behaviour
- Flexibility

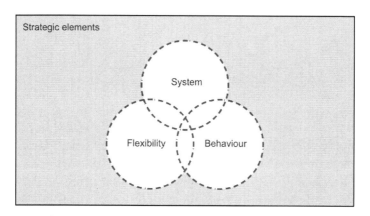

The basis for a solid strategy foundation is the playing style/formation. We will describe it in this chapter. In the Third Competence chapter, we will look at how the manager uses it to create behaviour. And in the Fourth Competence chapter we will describe why flexibility is extremely important in order to achieve success.

The difference between football and business
Discussing strategy foundation is very important in relation to the business world. In football, the distance between system and behaviour is rather small. The answers are known beforehand, and the expectation of you as a manager is that you win every single time. The goal is quite simply to win as many matches as possible. Nothing more or less.

In the world of football, the professional manager has the advantage that most players have grown up close to football. They know the key play systems/formations and know the implications of each system. Football players have grown up knowing formations such as 4-4-2 or 4-5-1. From early on, we recognise team structures and the responsibility of each position on the pitch. Many of the basic patterns of dribbling, passing and running into position we have known since we were 6-8 years old. It is a huge advantage learning as a child rather than as an adult. Children acquire knowledge and behavioural patterns in totally different ways than grown-ups. The professional manager also has the advantage that most of his players have turned their hobby into a living and therefore have a big personal drive.

The world of business is not that fortunate. Here, it is often difficult to identify the "right" goals and even more difficult to measure if you are heading in the right direction or not. Companies are very different and operate in different industries. They have different organisational structures and work processes. This means a company cannot simply take for granted that a new employee knows the work processes and systems. And therefore it is impossible to expect new staff to know the industry, organisation and work process.

Today, huge sums are spent on developing company strategies, identifying goals and implementing strategies. But the implementation of strategies can be a tremendous challenge to companies because they are often large, have many departments and are physically spread over many locations. Many companies thus "forget" or do not have the resources necessary to transform strategy into action and behaviour.

It is obvious that transparency and fierce competition in professional football leagues create clear goals and that managers know what to expect if they do not deliver results. But that is exactly why we should try to learn from professional football. As managers we should ask ourselves the question how to create transparency, clear goals and clear evaluation criteria. This creates efficiency, which again creates results.

Why is the strategy foundation important?

The strategy or basic system should be known and rehearsed by all team players and managers should ensure that everyone agrees what must happen and when it must happen. In other words, the system must guarantee coordination of "time" and "space".

But there are other important reasons why the system should be practised beforehand:

- *Firstly:* When the match begins and the action is developing rapidly on the pitch, it is easy for the manager to lose what we would call his "overview" of proceedings. The system should ensure that players can execute the strategy successfully on their own.

- *Secondly,* a professional manager faces the challenge that he is given the worst seat in the entire stadium. He is positioned at ground-level and has a very bad visual view of the pitch. Not very unlike the challenge a business leader faces.

- *Thirdly,* once the game gets underway, it is almost impossible for a manager to coordinate the tactical game between the players. Therefore, each player must know precisely what is expected from him.

- *Finally,* a well-defined playing style/formation gives the manager a better chance to evaluate and revise the formation, the team and players individually. It gives him the opportunity to consider if he has to adjust the system, if players fit into the system or if he needs to purchase other profiles.

These challenges are very similar to the challenges business leaders face. When, on a daily basis, we get new tasks that require our attention and rapid response, it is easy to lose our overview of the bigger picture. Many leaders have, like the football manager, an unclear view from their "chair". Often, business leaders are not involved in individual work processes, and their teams may be physically far away or work during different hours. The lack of overview gets even worse depending on the complexity of the work and number of employees to take care of. The business leader will not be able to take part in all processes at all times, and that creates a need for a system, delegation and coaching.

Having a *system* is essential to both the football manager and the business leader. The manager wins more matches with a well-founded system. And the business leader can use a well-founded system to plan complex work processes, production flow, sales functions and so on.

It is difficult to run a business ideally if suppliers constantly deliver too late, if the production facility's three shifts do not function as expected, or if middle management thinks the goal is sales rather than profit.

The strategy and formation must be 100 percent rehearsed. It should be as natural as talking or breathing.

Strategy foundation

There are five basic elements needed for a solid strategy foundation:

- Explain why
- Define the strategy and system
- Explain the individual's role in relation to the team
- Establish responsibility and loyalty
- Make it simple

The interesting thing about these five basic elements is that they are totally independent of the chosen strategy. It does not matter if the manager chooses to use a defensive style, counter-attack or adopt the Dutch "total football" approach.

Explain why

One of the most important prerequisites for creating a strategy foundation is simply to explain "why".

By explaining the reasons behind a strategy and a playing style/formation, a manager achieves a number of things. Firstly it enables him to show his players what he thinks is important, and *why*. This increases the chances of players feeling motivated and committed. Players will get a sense of how, and according to what criteria, they will be evaluated.

Depending on the individual manager, there are different ways to explain "why". Some managers prefer to do it broadly across the team, while others prefer to talk to a few key players who may act as "ambassadors" to the rest of the team. In any case it is important that each player knows why he must do as instructed. Otherwise, the manager may easily be in a situation where he only has nine or ten players on his team, when in reality there are 11 players on the pitch.

Inclusion is an important element when explaining "why". In both football and business there are some positions and functions that naturally attract more attention than others. Often strikers get more attention because they score the goals. In business it may be the marketing people or perhaps the sales force. Nonetheless, it is important that defenders and midfield players understand how important it is that they deliver the ball to the strikers in the right way. In order to achieve maximum performance it is essential that all players are motivated and know why they must do as they are told to do.

In football it is also important what players do when they are not in control of the ball. Strikers or midfield players might have important roles using their running patterns. By going to the middle of the field or towards the edge of it they can create space for the man with possession or make other players available. It is extremely important to explain to every player how important these running patterns are.

Two very different football players who were, and are, really good at this are Lars Bastrup and Didier Drogbar. **Lars Bastrup** used to play for the Danish national side and Hamburg Sport-Verein during the 1970s and early 1980s, and he was very skilled at dragging the defenders with him, thereby creating space for his team mates. **Didier Drogbar**, who plays for Chelsea, is good at using his body to drag himself away from the defenders a few seconds before the crucial passes occur. This poses a dilemma to the defenders. Either they follow Drogbar and mark him, or they stay with the player in possession of the ball and allow Drogbar to drag himself free in preparation for a pass.

Football teaches us that it is just as important what you do when you are not in possession of the ball as when you are. In the world of business, we can help employees become more productive, even though they may not be at the centre of attention at a given moment or be temporarily unoccupied. In some work places, for example, there are whole plans for what employees should do if they are idle. It might be an employee at a fast-food restaurant knowing that with no customers around the first priority is cleaning the place. Second priority could be to restock shelves in the kitchen. Third priority might involve checking on the toilets and so on. As a business leader, this ensures that an employee with spare time contributes in a positive way to the rest of the team and the production.

In business we tend to focus on goals and processes, but forget to explain why something is important and how things are interconnected. This despite the fact that as leaders we know that employees are much more motivated when they are passionate and have in-depth knowledge of their work. To most people there is nothing more discouraging than not knowing how their job fits into the overall scheme of things and how their performance is viewed by their managers. This can be a very unpleasant experience for an employee.

This is not at all unlike the current situation within the education and health sectors, where employees are continuously forced to spend more and more time on administrative processes. Whether you agree or disagree with the new processes, it does not seem as though any real effort has been made to explain why these specific processes are important. The general view probably is that many of these administrative processes "steal" time from the central goals of the job, namely teaching or taking care of the sick and elderly.

Politicians and civil servants can legally make sure procedures are adhered to, but it is doubtful they will gain acceptance of this without trying to explain "why".

Define the strategy and system

With the background for, and explanation of, the strategy and system already in place it is important that they are defined. The goal is not to define the strategy and system for the sake of the manager, but more for the sake of the team as a whole and the individual players.

Often it will be an advantage to define the strategy and system as simple as possible. This makes it far easier for the players to understand the strategy and the system. It also makes it easier to turn the strategy and system into the desired behaviour on the field.

A common understanding of the strategy and system is the basis for creating a tightly-knit team. A team that can act dynamically and as a unit. This is the setting players need to make decisions when they are on the pitch. Not only on the ball, but off the ball as well. The team will gain a full understanding of what is required of them as a team.

Many managers work closely with key players who make up the core of the team. When older players leave the club, or new players arrive, it is easier to maintain the strategy and system because the remaining players already have a clear understanding of them. It becomes easier for the manager and the team to create continuity and stability regarding the team's playing style/formation.

The importance of communicating the strategy and system is evident in for example Italian clubs. They often have a broad team with many players of a high level technically capable of replacing any one of the 11 men on the field. Italian clubs use this strength by continuously replacing players in action. It is said that many Italian clubs boast reserve players that would be part of the fixed teams of other clubs. This flexibility also creates a fierce competition within the individual clubs. As a player, you need to be on top all the time or you will quickly be relegated to the bench.

Explain the individual's role in relation to the team

All managers know that a team is made up of individuals. A big challenge is to make each player understand and accept his role as part of the team. Nonetheless, one of the most important tasks of a manager or business leader is to make sure that each player or employee understands exactly what their role is in relation to the team and what the team expects from them.

This understanding of individual roles is central to a successful team in three ways:

- First of all, the individual player needs to understand his own role in the team. As an example, a midfielder's role in defence might be to mark a specific opponent and in offence to provide deep passes to the strikers.

- Secondly, each player must understand the other players' roles. Using the example of the midfielder, it is important that he understands that the defensive marking of a specific opponent helps the defence destroy the opposition's attack. At the same time the midfielder must know the attacking side's running patterns when it is time for deep passes.

- Thirdly, each player must know how the individual roles fit into the overall system. If, for example, you play counter football, midfielders should not hold on to the ball but pass it on to strikers using long passes.

Most people, during their careers, will change department or employer several times. The first weeks or even months in a new position can be tough and a huge transformation. This is because we do not know our new role and the new colleagues' roles. We do not know the individual work processes, and we are uncertain of the criteria on which we are being evaluated. In the world of business we probably have a tendency to tell ourselves that new employees will acclimatise themselves and that established colleagues will guide the new ones toward their right place. But as the older colleagues were themselves trained in the same way, we can probably do a lot better when it comes to delegating roles and creating understanding.

Establish responsibility and loyalty

Responsibility and loyalty are key ingredients in order for a manager to create success.

Responsibility and loyalty can be built in many ways, but it requires that players have a clear understanding of their own role in relation to the rest of the team. When a manager defines roles, mutual understanding and loyalty is often created. But the manager has to implement systems and processes capable of solving possible conflicts between the individual roles. The risks of defining roles too precisely are that players believe this gives them free access to criticise each other. If a team loses, for example, it is not uncommon that defenders will criticise strikers for scoring too few goals, while strikers maintain that the defenders allowed too many goals against them. Therefore it is extremely important that the manager is able to control and solve conflicts. Several managers have, wholly or partially, introduced a "no blame" culture. This means players are not allowed to criticise each other, or perhaps only under certain circumstances.

The "no blame" culture does not mean, however, that players are not being reviewed. And it does not imply that players cannot criticise or expect things from each other. What it does mean is that it is much more important that the team, in an objective way, can discuss each others' roles and the challenges they face. You might call it to "go for the ball" instead of "go for the man". **Arsene Wenger** is known for having introduced a "no blame" culture to his strikers. The strikers were not allowed to be criticised in public as it is often easy to attack a striker on a bad streak, particularly if the team has lost many matches.

In the world of business we very often focus on the individual performance, which is indeed important. But we often criticise the individual if the *process* is not working well instead of making it a team discussion to find out why it is not working and what to do to solve the situation.

Make it simple

The last important element needed to create a strong strategy foundation is to focus on doing things in a simple, even simplistic, way. Managers and business leaders will obtain a number of advantages by doing things in a simple way:

- The strategy and system become easier to remember.
- It makes it easier for the individual player or employee to understand his or her role.
- It makes it easier for the individual player or employee to understand colleagues' roles.
- It makes it easier to remember and execute the simple playing style/formation or the individual work process.
- It increases the chances that the system or work process becomes as natural a thing as talking or breathing.
- It increases the amount of flexibility.

The last element (flexibility) is often the difference between success and failure. In the world of football, as in the world of business, it can be difficult to foresee the competition's next move. Many managers and business leaders know from experience that the solution is not to come up with a plan for every possible scenario. Neither manager nor players can absorb this. Besides, the future is not always what we thought it would be. That is why flexibility is essential. It is far easier to be flexible when you have a simple formation instead of a complex one.

In Denmark in recent years, there has been a lot of discussion about national team manager **Morten Olsen**'s very tight formation of the team. There is little doubt that the system is entertaining and that the Danes has a lot of ball possession. Critics, however, believe the formation is used for the sake of the formation, and that players are selected based on this. No matter what you feel about Morten Olsen's system it will surely be an advantage if the systems can be adjusted to different situations during matches, allowing players from time to time to play a more opportunistic role.

Conclusion

From the world of football we know how important an understanding of strategy and system is. Professional managers and business leaders face the same challenges when it comes to creating understanding and acceptance of their strategies and systems. This is often a prerequisite for building motivation and commitment.

The challenge is not made any easier by the fact that the manager and the business leader often get the worst seat available at the "stadium". Neither the manager nor the business leader has much say on the individual processes when the game is under way. Therefore a strong strategy foundation is necessary.

As a business leader, these key points will give you an advantage:

- Create a strong strategy foundation – it increases chances of success.
- Create a strong strategy foundation – it ensures a systematic approach to evaluation and change.
- Define the strategy and system – not for your own sake, but so the entire team understands them.
- Always begin by explaining "why" – if not it will be difficult to gain acceptance and support.
- Always explain to each individual what his or her role is.
- Always explain to each individual what the others' roles are.
- Explain what others expect from each individual.
- Make sure everyone is loyal to the system and the team.
- Make sure the system is simple – this increases flexibility.

We believe that business leaders should allocate both time and resource to explaining "why" to their employees. The worst thing that can happen is that you will encounter understanding, committed and loyal employees. And that is hardly the worst beginning of a new project or strategy.

Advantages and learning

Besides the fact that behaviour determines the team's fate on the pitch, there are a number of important and instant advantages of being able to turn strategy and system into specific behaviour. These advantages have been described in the official FA guide to "Basic Team Coaching".[18]

The advantages of being able to turn strategy and system into behaviour are:

- creating a natural and efficient behaviour
- saving time in the heat of the match
- ensuring the entire team speaks the same "language"
- creating confidence and a sense of advantage.

First of all, a continued physical repetition of playing styles and formations will ensure that the strategy and system become natural, even automatic, to the players.

Secondly, the team will be able to save so many valuable seconds in thousands of situations throughout a season when players have to decide who to pass to and where to position themselves and run on the pitch.

The third advantage is that players will speak the same "language". That is, they will be on the same level with a shared understanding of what they are trying to achieve and how they will achieve it when setting foot on the pitch.

Finally, well-rehearsed strategies and systems create confidence and a sense of advantage for the players. A team with a plan will feel stronger and more confident to face the challenges of the game and will have an increased sense of having the situation under control. If the system is good, it will also give players a mental edge and a feeling of being on top of the game.

There are four basic techniques and approaches to turning strategy and system into specific behaviour. Most professional managers will use all four techniques to a greater or lesser degree.

The four basic learning techniques:

- Repetitive training.
- Training of specific details.
- Training of behaviour that is intuitively illogical.
- Training of what to do when not in possession of the ball.

Repetitive training

The fundamental purpose of repetitive training is to entrench all the basic behavioural patterns of the system played. The behaviours are practised over and over until they are deeply rooted. The repetitive training ensures that the team knows the system intimately. This again guarantees that the team as a whole has the ability to respond rapidly and knows what to do in a given situation. This common understanding of the system and the defined behaviours contributes to creating a feeling of confidence. The team will feel that they have been in this situation before and can handle it comfortably.

Repetitive training can be observed at Italian football club SS Lazio. It is no coincidence that manager **Delio Rossi** (manager 2005-2009) makes his players train running and passing patterns again and again, hour after hour.[19]

There is a significant difference regarding the focus on repetitive training in professional football and business. In the world of football this part often plays a large role during an entire training season. The professional manager will begin to coach the new system right from the pre-season training. And players will be trained and adjusted throughout the entire season. In the world of business, the approach is often the opposite. In most companies, most of the time is spend on the "pitch" – doing the work. At the very best, employees are from time to time sent on a course or a training programme. It is, however, more the exception than the rule that training of the work processes is left to the individual and his or her colleagues. In business, we rely on on-the-job training to deliver the results.

Nonetheless, there are some industries that spend a lot of time on training and follow-up. This is the case for professions such as pilots, doctors and accountants. The most obvious comparison, however, would be professional performers such as professional ballet dancers and opera singers who spend a large part of the season rehearsing their roles. The number of performances is relatively few.

Training of specific details

Professional football managers and their assistants use enormous resources training specific part-elements of their strategy and system.

First of all, this makes it possible to coach with a certain amount of continuity. Instead of exposing the team to a long and maybe complicated play situation, the manager will isolate a specific detail that can be trained over and over again during a short period of time. This makes it possible for players to understand the specific details thoroughly and gives the manager a chance to explain "why" in relation to the strategy and system.

Football managers also use this technique when training elements that are particularly difficult or require additional focus. This could be a set-piece situation, which statistics show is one of the most important factors in deciding whether you win or lose a match. Or it might be particularly demanding or difficult passes that need to be trained.

The most important element about training specific details may be that it boosts the team's morale. If the manager insists, right from the beginning of the season, on training the *entire* system and all possible combinations, the team will quickly get tired. By training part-elements the team and the individual players achieve small victories. They see that the playing style/formation works and that they can handle it.

As soon as the manager is happy with the handling of the individual elements, he can begin bringing them together. This might be very specific things such as passing patterns between midfield and attack. Large elements can be brought together as well, for example the transformation from defensive play to counter football.

Compare this to the world of business, where this kind of attention to detail in training is rare. With the exception of a few specific sectors, it is *very* rare in business to train specific details hour after hour, day after day. Because of this, we do not always achieve the desired skills and natural execution.

Training of behaviour that is intuitively illogical

There are many processes or behavioural patterns in football and the world of business that do not seem logical right away. This is very central to the football world.

From an early age young football players learn how to engage in trivial tasks that go against our instincts. It might be heading the ball when it is passed to them at a high speed. It could be tackling a player twice their size. Or making sure their body is over the ball when they strike – otherwise the ball will miss the goal. But there are much greater boundaries that need to be crossed.

One of the most difficult things to learn for very young players is to pass the ball into empty space – that is, being able to anticipate where the receiver of the ball will be during the split second it takes the ball to pass through the air. There is nothing more frustrating to a striker than getting the ball behind you or at the place you were half a second ago. The striker ideally needs to receive the ball in front of him so he can dribble or kick at full speed.

This kind of training rarely occurs in the world of business. Surgeons learn that it is okay to cut into people. Pilots learn to fly by instruments, without using their visual or physical orientation. But in many companies these learning processes are left to the employees to master on their own.

Training of what to do when not in possession of the ball

The last important training technique in football is coaching behaviours which ensure that those players not in possession of the ball are productive as well.

Most managers will have a more or less constant focus on what players are doing when they are not in possession of the ball. This is totally logical, because while there are 11 people on a football team, only one of them has, or ought to have, the ball at any given time. Ideally, the person with ball possession will always have 4-5 team mates he can pass on to. But this requires that the other team members are constantly changing position relative to the opposing team (and to the person who has the ball). It will obviously be disastrous if a football team has trained the wrong running patterns or – even worse – the players do not move around enough. This puts the player in possession of the ball under unnecessary pressure and increases the risk of losing the ball.

A player not in possession of the ball may be productive in many ways. Firstly, he should position himself correctly in relation to the general situation on the pitch – for example, if the team is on the offensive, the midfield will naturally move further ahead on the pitch. Secondly, he can draw the other side's players away from the ball, therefore ensuring more free space for the player in possession of the ball.

Finally, and perhaps most importantly, he can make himself free and available for passes from the player with ball possession.

In the world of business it can be somewhat more difficult to differentiate between the person in possession of the ball and the person who needs to run into position. But when talking about projects it is basically necessary to ensure that the specific work processes are running as smoothly and efficiently as possible. For a good description of these processes, see *M. Hammer and J. Champy: Reengineering the Coporation*.[20] The essence of this book is to focus on optimising the process from the perspective of the customer and the expected buying process.

Most companies, even today, are still organised on the basis of traditional departmental principles. The accounting department needs to be able to refer profit and cost to specific parts of the process. This means that the company is divided into professional or technical silos: Sales department, production, finance department, legal department... As an example, a company like this may have a sales department selling products, a financial department calculating sales offers and a legal department checking the financial situation of the customer. When the company "produces", this information passes from one silo to another. And this often causes loss of important information and time.

Hammer and Campy's point is that the customer did not buy one "sales department", one "financial department" and one "legal department". The customer bought a product, and then the rest is pretty much irrelevant. The company therefore might consider training the sales people to be able to perform all three functions, letting the customer get his sales offer and order confirmation right away. And the sales person might be able to send the order via a mobile unit and get offers and approval in a matter of minutes.

The training of what you as a player or employee do while not in possession of the "ball" draws a number of parallels to the just-in-time principle. Basically, it is about timing. The ball and the product need to be moved around in the most efficient way. It does not help that strikers are in the right position if the ball is not there. And it is useless that a sales person is in the middle of a meeting with a buyer ready to sign the contract if the products are not deliverable. On the other hand, it is also a waste if the ball or the product arrive too early.

Conclusion

If they are honest, most business leaders will probably admit that they have at least once presented a goal and strategy without turning it into specific behaviour. Professional football can show how we in business can train and develop behaviours. A professional football manager has just one focus, which is to use all possible means to optimise the team's behaviour on the pitch. Strategy without the right behaviour has no merit.

As a business leader, you can apply the following principles to improve behaviours in your organisation:

- Turn strategy into behaviour.
- Learn strategy – it saves time, creates efficiency, a common language and confidence.
- Train the most important part-elements over and over again.
- Train elements that intuitively seem illogical – they may be crucial.
- Train your department or company so it can act when not in possession of the "ball".

Rounding off this chapter, the following is a quote from a young graffiti artist:

"Words without action are indifferent."

THE FOURTH COMPETENCE
MAKE YOUR STRATEGY FLEXIBLE

On 29 November 2007, Danish side AaB was up against Tottenham Hotspur at White Hart Lane during the group stages of the UEFA Cup. It was to be an entertaining and atypical match in many ways. No less than five goals would be scored during those 2x45 minutes.

Already before the match there had been a lot of speculation. The proud English club had less than a month earlier signed the world's most expensive manager contract with Sevilla FC manager **Juande Ramos**. He had only had a handful of matches in charge of Tottenham before the encounter with AaB. The great challenge was, and is, for Juande Ramos to get firm control of the club, which had for so many seasons found itself at the middle of the Premier League.

AaB's Swedish manager, **Erik Hamren**, before the match said it was the biggest challenge for the club during his reign as manager. If his side were to pull a draw against Tottenham on away ground it would be a sensational result for AaB.

In the evening of 29 November 2007, Tottenham and AaB finally clashed at White Hart Lane. When, after just two minutes of play, Thomas Enevoldsen took AaB ahead by 1-0, it was obvious that this match would not progress as expected. A sensational upset was in prospect. During the next 35 minutes, AaB controlled more and more of the match, and sometimes it looked as if Tottenham's defence was going to disintegrate. In the 38th minute, Kasper Risgård increased AaB's lead to 2-0.

During the break, Tottenham manager Juande Ramos decided to replace Lee Young-Pyo and Jarmaine Jenas with Tom Huddlestone and Darren Bent respectively, and this would prove crucial.

Just two minutes into the second half, Huddlestone made a pass to an available Berbatov, who reduced AaB's lead to 1-2. And three minutes later Huddlestone again made a great pass to Robbie Keane, who secured the equalising 2-2.

Tottenham had given AaB the same shock start that they themselves had suffered during the first half. And after twenty minutes of play, Tottenham's Darren Bent more or less closed the game with a goal. 3-2 to Tottenham.

If reality turns outs different than planned...

In order to achieve success, your strategy needs to be flexible, and as manager you need to think opportunistically. It is not enough that a manager knows how to develop strategy and system and turn the strategy into behaviour. The manager, the system and the players need to be able to act flexibly.

If the strategy and system do not work, they need to be optimised during the two times 45 minutes a football match lasts. You need to find a solution.

In the example of AaB and Tottenham, both managers had to revise their initial system and adjust to reality on the pitch.

AaB assumed from the beginning that the match would be very tough and that a draw would be a huge success for the club. And when Hamren saw that the Tottenham defence was insecure, he only had to adjust the strategy and keep putting the pressure on. In the same way, Juande Ramos had to admit that his system and team did not cope at all during the first half. He therefore wisely decided to replace two players during the halftime break.

Flexibility is a necessity in order to win

Flexibility is a necessity in modern football. Planning and preparations before a match will never keep pace with the actual developments. The manager or business leader therefore obviously needs to follow the action closely and think opportunistically if given the chance.

Modern football poses two great paradoxes when it comes to flexibility:

- It is a paradox that a well-established playing system/ formation may actually undermine success (if not flexible).
- It is a paradox that a well-established playing system/ formation is the prerequisite for creating great flexibility.

During the season, a football team is confronted with hundreds of unforeseen situations. It could be a team playing with different formations, injury among players, replacements, selling of players or red and yellow cards.

It is extremely difficult to develop a system capable of handling so many different situations. Besides, the manager and the players face the challenge that many unforeseen situations occur during a match. Often, it is difficult for the manager to communicate with players during the match, and the halftime break is therefore vitally important if you need to make major adjustments. The manager's other main challenge is that he is only allowed to use three substitutes during a match, and this limits how many adjustments he can make to the team.

Systems are a prerequisite for flexibility

The term "flexibility" from a management perspective is often misunderstood. Flexibility frequently becomes an excuse for not having made plans or created a fixed environment.

Efficient flexibility needs a fixed environment and often great planning. If you work with flexibility *without* a fixed environment it may, in the worst case, lead to chaos, frustration and financial loss.

Efficient flexibility is built on fixed systems. This means that a manager or business leaders must ensure that everyone understands:

- Which elements of the system need to be changed.
- Which elements should not be changed.

If the basic system is not in place, we will have a situation where players are unsure which elements have been changed and which will not be changed.

Professional football managers have long been aware that the basic system is the foundation for being flexible. When all players have the same understanding of the system and know exactly why each single element is important, it becomes much easier to specify what changes are needed and how to implement them.

The point of creating a balance between system and flexibility is that the players retain their deep knowledge of the basic system. It is mentally easier to face changing one or two elements in a system if you know that the remaining 95 percent will stay the way they have already been learned.

In the world of business we have a lot to learn from this point. For many companies the fact that they use on-the-job training is often an excuse for not having fixed and well-learned systems. It is easier to have a current employee pass on his own systems to a new recruit than to train them. When there are no fixed systems, the individual employee has to create a system himself. This becomes a problem when many employees develop each their own systems. The business leader then has a very small chance of creating efficiency and even less chance of making important changes to the strategy.

It is therefore crucial to spend a lot of time explaining "why" and making sure the strategy is implemented in a way that results in the desired behaviours.

Simple systems are more flexible

Most managers agree that simple systems often provide greater flexibly and thus success. Simple systems have a great many advantages when it comes to flexibility. Basically, a simple system means that:

- The system is easy to remember.
- The system is easy to execute.

- Everyone on the team understands the system.
- The manager can spend time coaching the system rather than spending time explaining it.
- Simple systems create familiarity.

A football team and manager need to make thousands of decisions during a long season with many matches. It is almost impossible to create enough systems to deal with all these situations. And it is even more difficult for a team to learn and remember all these systems. Efficient flexibility thus requires a simple playing style/formation that can be adjusted without limits

As an example, former Ajax Amsterdam manager **Ronald Koeman** used two basic systems. As a point of departure, he used an offensive system in the Dutch Eredivisie and a more offensive system in European championships.[21] Ronald Koeman was very prescient and created two systems that in reality had great similarity. This ensured that the players benefited from great familiarity with the systems and a lot of play time using them. Both systems, for example, used a flat defence chain with four defenders and many common features in the midfield and attack. The difference was rather how fast the team had to adjust when they lost or won a ball. Ronald Koeman made Ajax Amsterdam national champions twice, and the team also won the Dutch cup tournament.

Avoid changes to the basic system

Any manager wants to avoid being in a situation where the strategy and basic system themselves do not work – where the team's systems consistently do not live up to the manager's or team's expectations.

When a manager changes the strategy and basic system it means that many variables are activated. The players suddenly need to face not just one or two adjustments to their regular playing style, but a fundamental shift. They may soon find themselves in a position where they do not know "why" and "how" the new system is best played; they are not familiar with the positions and passing play; they remain behind the opposing side all the time.

The art of being opportunistic

Being flexible also implies that the manager needs to think opportunistically. That is, the manager should not only evaluate and decide on a given situation, but to a much larger extent get the team to create the desired situations.

This was evident in the example of AaB and Tottenham earlier in this chapter. AaB kept on putting pressure on Tottenham during the entire first half when first they realised that the opponent's defence was weak. Of course it is difficult to specify exactly when a manager needs to stick to the basic system and when to be opportunistic. As an example, Brazil's manager during the 2002 World Cup, **Luiz Felipe Scolari**, was very opportunistic in his strategy. The team was changed from match to match, and the line-up and system were optimised throughout the entire tournament.

Managers will often act opportunistically if they know that a player from the opposing side is not 100 percent ready or may play in an unfamiliar position. They can take advantage by using the team's existing system, but adjusting slightly to put additional pressure on the player in question.

During the fall of 2007, an interesting discussion from a management perspective came up. The Danish national team had missed the qualification for the 2008 European Championship final round, and manager **Morten Olsen** received a lot of criticism for his choice of playing style/formation and players. For instance, Olsen said that Kenneth Perez was not suitable for the playing style/formation despite that fact that he is one of the most successful Danish players abroad.[22]

Whether you agree with the criticism of Morten Olsen or not it is a fact that Denmark did not qualify for the 2008 European Championship. Needless to say, as a professional manager Olsen will consider whether to make marginal changes in the time ahead, whether individual players in specific positions do not perform satisfactorily, or if it might be the basic system that does not work.

Observe, Evaluate, Act

Because of the enormous pressure placed on professional managers, most of them have learned that they need to be focused on action rather than hesitation. The reason is that the expectations are that the team wins each match, so the manager basically has to start all over every time. Every time a match is played, the manager only has 2x45 minutes to judge if he should make changes or not. As only victory counts, in many national leagues and tournaments it is insignificant by how many goals you lose. A manager therefore needs to be willing to make decisions and take the necessary chances in order to win.

Football is, for good and bad, a "right here, right now" sport. This means that changes and implementation need to be dynamic and follow the development of a game or the season. The question of flexibility and system is deeply rooted in the consciousness of the manager during every season, every match and every half. The manager will constantly face three factors:

- **Observe – Evaluate – Act**
- *Observe:* How is the actual situation developing?
- *Evaluate:* Is the basic strategy working, and what does this imply?
- *Act:* Which marginal changes must be made?

The professional football manager will cope with reality and the actual situation in a matter-of-fact way. He will continuously evaluate whether the basic strategy is efficient and produce the desired results. He will evaluate the consequences of changing or not changing the system. And finally, the manager will evaluate which marginal changes should be made.

Conclusion

In the business world we can use the football managers' experience with, and understanding of, flexibility as a source of inspiration on many levels.

First of all we can learn that well-trained systems are the foundation needed in order to make efficient changes on a busy daily basis. Just as important, we can learn that we, as business leaders, have to differentiate between marginal and fundamental changes to the system.

As a business leader, the following points will be useful:

- Do not turn flexibility into an excuse for not planning.
- Only make marginal changes as long as the basic system is working.
- Always define what is changed and what remains unchanged.
- As the point of departure use a simple system that can be varied endlessly.
- Carefully consider when it may pay off to be opportunistic.
- Observe and evaluate continuously in order to assess if you need to make marginal or structural changes.

THE FIFTH COMPETENCE
FIND THE RIGHT PEOPLE

In 2002, Brazil's **Ronaldo** was sold to Real Madrid for 39 million Euros. In 1996, PSV Eindhoven had paid six million dollars for the same player. That is a twelvefold increase of his market value! And not unwarranted, since Ronaldo has accomplished winning both the World Cup and being named World Player of the Year.[23]

During the 2000/2001 season, PSV Eindhoven's **Van Nistelrooy** was sold to England's Manchester United for 19 million pounds Sterling. Just two years before, Eindhoven had bought him for 6.3 million Euros. His value had more than quadrupled. Not a bad deal, and quite deservedly so, as Van Nistelrooy scored 23 goals in 32 matches during his first season in England and claimed the record as the Premier League player with most scored goals in several matches in a row.[24]

What if these players had not been spotted? And who noticed them before others?

Both players were spotted, and to a certain extent developed, by talent scout **Frank Arnesen**, at that time attached to PSV Eindhoven. Who is Frank Arnesen, and what makes him capable of spotting such huge potential and qualities in talented players?

Frank Arnesen became famous back in the 1980s when playing for the Danish national side, completing 52 international matches. Besides being a fixture of the Danish team during the 1980s, he has worked professionally in clubs such as Danish Fremad Amager, Dutch side Ajax Amsterdam, Spain's Valencia, RSC Anderlecht of Belgium and finally PSV Eindhoven of the Netherlands.

Following his career as an active player, Frank Arnesen first became assistant manager under **Bobby Robson** at PSV Eindhoven.

He later became sports manager in the same club and helped spot and develop players such as Ronaldo and Van Nistelrooy.

This talent for spotting and developing talented players later brought him to Chelsea, where today he is head of development.

What is it exactly that talent scouts such as Frank Arnesen look for? And how do they work when spotting talents for future major clubs?

What is talent? The complete player – the complete human being!

During our research and interviews with talent scouts, managers and former top players, most have been evasive when having to answer the question: "What is talent?" But when pressed for an answer, most of them have come up with pretty similar definitions and descriptions. We will get back to the reason for this evasiveness later.

The answer may be quite obvious, as most interviewees pointed out that a talented player is a player who is more gifted or competent than most other players – standing out from the crowd! And when speaking of football, we most often found the following criteria for being gifted, although the precise formula for "talent" is naturally rather complex.

Generally speaking, these competences are divided into two main groups, namely functional competences and social competences:

- *Functional competences*

    - Physique or potential physique (for example endurance, sprint and speed, often depending on the stature of the player).

    - Feeling for the ball/technique (for example skills such as dribbling, kicking and passing).

- Positioning and "eye for the game" (for example the ability to position yourself according to team players and opponents as well as an understanding of tactics).

- *Social competences*

  - Temper, expressed in many ways, as temper often means a strong will or capability to self-motivate.

  - Courage and willpower, a vague term, but often described as a willingness to fight hardship on and off the pitch – for example if you are down by several goals against a stronger team or are suffering from an injury.

  - Communication and cooperation with team players and the manager. These skills are often described as clear and unambiguous communication, but interestingly also as ᵃᵐᵖathic – that is, engaging communication where the strengthens the ties between himself and his team . The opposite can and should, however, often also ᵉsent. For example the ability to pose challenging but ᵘuctive demands to team mates and the team in ᵃl, including the manager.

presents our analytical decoding of our own he talent scouts generally came up with a slightly r: completeness! That is, the complete human being. The complete talent. And here it is probably worth mentioning that in this chapter we are looking at raw talent and not the groomed star player who has already proved his worth through his matches and results (spotting the latter rarely requires great insight, but simply a large investment!).

Whether you are scouting for a defender, a goalkeeper, a midfielder or a striker, in the world of football you are almost always looking for completeness, even if the player is not perfect or needs to improve in certain areas in order to fulfil his talent.

The talent scout looks for both strengths and weaknesses at the same time in order to understand the complete player. They know all too well that even though some players may have developed their skills to a much greater level than other players of the same age, many of these apparent stars-in-the-making will get overtaken by others yet-to-be-developed players. It is therefore important that you scout for talent that needs to be developed and that you look at more than just the functional competences, looking rather at the complete talent – the complete human being!

Why this completeness? Because football is so complex that an analysis of specific competence in one area or another cannot in itself determine whether a talent can be fulfilled. This depends on the person and his personality, or rather his attitude towards, and participation in, the interaction he needs to be a part of: the team! Not unlike life in organisations and companies.

Realising this complex connection between the functional and social competences, most talent scouts use the rule of the thumb that if for example three in five necessary competences are present, and the remaining two might be developed to a respectable level, provided that both functional and social competences are shown, then most clubs will be interested in investing large sums on resources developing the talent.

In order not to invest in the wrong players, recruiting is a long process for most professional clubs. A process which is both formal and informal, because managers use a wide-ranging network of colleagues and observers to get independent intelligence about players on the field. Later on, the player may be invited to join a trial training session, trial matches, a trial period and a number of conversations as well as several health and physical examinations. These many elements of the screening process make up the frame of this picture of the complete human being – the complete talent!

The same lengthy thoroughness is very rarely seen in organisations outside the world of sport, although the process in principle could and should be the same.

A professional football club knows that both its short-term and long-term success sport-wise and financially depends on the ability to recruit the right players. That is why the role of talent scout is often elevated to a higher level in the clubs.

The same does not go for the last few decades of organisational development in the world of business. Here the trend has mostly been towards increasingly flat organisations with totally or partially outsourced HR and recruiting functions – even the scouting function!

Look at how hardship is handled – a good indicator!

Finding the right players is crucial to a club as well as a company.

But the scouting is complex. So instead of looking for immediate skills and competences present in the player – the typical functional talents that need to be present or at least capable of development – the talent scout will often focus on whether the player can be developed within a reasonable timeframe. And here social competences and personal characteristics will often be at the centre. Not least the ability to deal with hardship. There are many stories of newly recruited players spending months (or longer) playing on the reserve team, but because the manager and talent scout believed in their talent (including their social competences), the manager would keep them in the squad, and later they would blossom and eventually become star players in their own right – indeed being fixtures on the first team and national side!

Every talent scout and manager has their own yardstick and their own methods, but all of them will assess both technical ability and attitude, thereby creating a complete picture of the player and the human being behind the player. But if we have to sum up these elements in one thing, it is the ability to deal with adversity in a constructive manner – both on and off the pitch.

For example, how does the player react to a missed pass? What does he say? What does he do? How does he react to his own mistakes? Does he become sad and reserved or the exact opposite? These are the signs that the talent scout, consciously or unconsciously, uses to create a complete picture of the person. In this respect the world of football has a far more wide-ranging assessment process than the world of business, which does not always strive in the same way to get a thorough view of new recruits.

Who spots the talent?

It is obvious that competitive companies must recruit potential star performers in the same way as professional football clubs recruit new players.

Jim Collins, professor at Stanford School of Business, California[25], states that the most important factor in determining the success of an organisation (the first of his five basic factors) is deciding "who the company should bring along on the road to success."[26] Collins came to this conclusion after studying a vast number of successful and unsuccessful companies over a long period of time. Successful companies, like the best professional football clubs, spend many resources and a lot of time spotting, maintaining and developing their personnel and defining who should come along on the road to success for the company – the team!

Today, most companies do in fact know that having great employees – at least in key positions – is crucial, especially in a market situation characterised by increased competition.

But how do most companies then in fact go about spotting talented employees? Well, typically they do it by screening written applications. The normal policy is only to let the most "perfect" candidates get through, whereas the football talent scout knows that the perfect application does not necessarily prove the talent – this will only show during real action. Otherwise, the football talent scout would only be judging the functional competences, and we have seen that this is not the way they operate.

The world of business has made some moves in the right direction, and now often uses different kinds of psychological profile tests – but still after the initial pre-screening mentioned above. These psychological tests are meant to disclose an applicant's "indirect" competences, the social and personal characteristics. And the tests *are* becoming more and more advanced and better, although they are yet not fully developed or complete.

Using these tests, however, does not remove the basic problem – that they often show a picture of the candidate at this very moment in his or her current development progress, while giving very little indication of the potential for further development. And they do not give any indication at all (or very little) about the way the candidate will fit in with the team and the culture they will be joining – the workplace/team.

These competences are too often in the world of business only given cursory appraisal, and are assessed intuitively without any kind of control measures – and are considered at the very best in the final stage of the recruitment process.

So while in the world of business companies may *try* to create a rounded picture of a job candidate, the reality is that their assessment is often fragmented and incomplete – and in reality, much less varied and comprehensive than is the case in the world of professional football.

Intuition – from conscious repetition to unconscious perfection

Football's talent scouts, unlike the headhunters and human resources staff in the business world, are themselves a part of the players' daily life. They often join training sessions. And in particular they are often, as in the case of **Frank Arnesen**, former top players themselves. This means that, to a far greater extent than their counterparts in the business world, they are, or have been, actively involved in the sharp end of the "business". As a result they have a much greater understanding of the functional and social competences required.

In most companies, the human resources unit is a staff function with indirect responsibility for the company's results. Far too many headhunters remain, throughout most of their careers, human resource consultants, although of course some have proven success from earlier management functions. A recent British survey in

Management Today/Ceridian[27] seems to prove this, with almost 50 percent of employees believing that the human resource department does not contribute positively, and no less than 22 percent believing the contribution is negative!

Jack Welch, in his days as CEO of General Electric, once said that he would prefer it if his HR bosses had themselves had been "a part of the game". He believed that a person who had gained experience and success working with line management responsibility, for example in sales, marketing or production, could be turned into a capable HR manager with knowledge about those areas. Jack Welch thought that a good HR manager should understand the candidates about to be employed on a much deeper level than could be achieved through short interviews alone, and that they should not place undue reliance on superficial personality and skills tests. He believed the human resources manager should know instinctively when he is face to face with a player worth offering a job.

The competitive world of football seems to confirm Jack Welch's views. And this may also explain why the talent scouts who we interviewed, as earlier noted, often hesitated when asked to describe what they looked for in a prospective signing. Football talent scouts have spent years gathering football knowledge and have experienced numerous matches both as players and as spectators, which have provided them with insight and an intuitive understanding. The same is not always the case with the football talent scout's counterparts in the world of business, where it is positively unusual for recruiters to have enjoyed a long and successful technical career in the areas they are recruiting for.

Instant settlement in football – but what about the world of business?

Another thought-provoking fact when comparing football talent scouts with human resources professionals or headhunters relates to resale clauses or "kick-backs". Yes, this is what it is called in everyday language, and actually it has nothing to do with football.

Professional football club contracts vary widely from club to club and from individual to individual, but they often include a sort of royalty or payment that relates to the original club that spotted, invested in and developed the player at an early stage of the player's career – and this also goes for club change number two, three, four and so on. Quite a few small clubs have such contracts with their players, as the smaller leagues are widely considered a "breeding ground" providing players to Europe's biggest clubs in places such as Spain, UK, Germany and Italy.

Such clauses featuring "kick-backs" actually constitute a rather significant source of revenue for small clubs. And even though the "kick-back" money ends up in the pockets of the club rather than the club's individual talent scout who spotted the player in the first place, they are a very precise measurement for how efficient a club and its talent scouts are when it comes to spotting and developing players. A precise and instant measurement that companies often totally lack.

The same kind of unambiguous real measurement of value-added growth through recruitment by today's companies is unknown to us. Quite the opposite, most companies operate with stability goals such as: How fast do members of the staff come and leave? How much sick leave is taken? Or they compile "satisfaction reports" surveying existing employee attitudes. Some may undertake "competence mapping" to try to improve efficiency and productivity. But only very few companies analyse who left the company and why, to learn crucial lessons from the loss of personnel.

What did FC Barcelona think when triple Spanish champion **Michael Laudrup** left the club in 1994 to join Real Madrid only to win two more championships and become one of the few in the world who has secured five titles in a row? This has been a hot topic of conversation for years in the football community, both inside and outside Spain – but what about similar situations in the companies of the business world?

Because what good is it that stability is high, if players with a winning mentality and great competences leave the company – or are not attracted to it in the first place? The professional football club, no matter how small, at least makes sure that it makes use of its players while it has them and gets its expenses covered (wherever possible) when the players leave. Food for thought!

The importance of recruiting, nurturing and retaining the right personnel is crucial in any organisation. The role of talent scout or recruiter is vital. In business it is true that some headhunters and HR professionals in companies are being measured (and remunerated) on performance. But we do find it interesting that the extremely competitive world of professional football has a specific measurement of the HR function's value-added effect – that is, the talent scout's direct contribution, as reflected in ongoing royalties earned from future clubs.

The hidden jewel and the young lion

The world of football is complex, and so is the world of business. In both there is a need always to allow for exceptions and nuances. However, from the recruiter's point of view there is one simple distinction which we would like to draw attention to – the question of whether you are looking for young or experienced recruits, the question of youth versus experience.

Whether you are a talent scout in the football world, or a recruiter in the business world, one of the first decisions you will need to make will be this: are you looking for young recruits who are not yet fully developed, or for experienced recruits who have established skills?

Obviously, there are very different considerations, different pros and cons in either case.

The ability to want to learn – another good indicator

Very young players may be "hidden jewels" that do not yet appear to be obvious potential stars, whereas slightly older players can be described as "young lions" – players clearly capable of demonstrating their talent or functional competences. The evaluation and nourishment of these two types are looked at fundamentally differently in the world of football.

In the next chapter we will take a closer look at the development of talent once it has been spotted. But right now we will try to sum up some of the cases from the world of football that have caught our interest.

When you have to judge the very young players – the hidden jewels – you obviously have to look at the players' immediate talents, their functional talents. But especially when talking about this group of players, what you see may not be unambiguous. As an example, small players such as former Danish star **Allan Simonsen** can compensate for their small physique by developing their technique.

Therefore you often need to evaluate the hidden jewels according to indirect signs or indicators of latent ability. And here social and personal competences and characteristics become relevant.

The hidden jewel – the young player – is often judged based on small issues that cannot be withheld or hidden during the heat of the game. Examples could be:

- Shout (or no shout).
- Protest (or no protest).
- Communication and signs to fellow players.
- Communication with opponents.
- Communication with the referee.
- Communication with the manager.
- Praise or criticism of fellow players, the referee or manager.

These descriptive characteristics are then, together with the specific functional characteristics, put together to provide a complete picture of the player, depending on whether the talent scout is on the hunt for a goalkeeper, defender, midfielder or striker. Using this picture, the talent scout decides whether the player is already better than the average or, at least as important, the player has the potential to maintain or develop his skills at a level above the average. And this is difficult, because who is the hidden jewel?

Most talent scouts spot players that stand out from the crowd because of their skills on the pitch – positive skills, that is. This is obvious. But after this, the talent scout will judge if the player can improve in other areas in order to become a real talent. And this is where business leaders have something to learn from the skilful talent scout and football manager.

One condition required is that the player needs to be focused and willing to learn. So when for example the manager asks players to pay attention to a certain area, the "hidden jewels" will understand quickly, and try immediately to follow the instruction. This remains the case even if they fail at first, because they *will* fail from time to time just like everyone else. But if the desire to improve, and the pleasure this brings with it, are there, this is often the prerequisite for potential to be realised. Arsenal's **Arsene Wenger** says he looks for *intelligent* players – players who in no time can and will learn from their mistakes, and who execute the outcome in their play.[28]

This is quite similar to the situation with management functions in many workplaces where the conscious and good leader – just like the talent scout or the football manager – should be able to see if an employee shows enthusiasm, even though not all functional skills are ready yet. Often, this is more valuable than immediate competences.

The young lion

With young lions (the older talents), the situation is somewhat different. Here, the player needs to be fully developed and ready to create results immediately using the functional competences, which therefore puts added focus on these competences.

In reality, this is simple. Has the young lion performed well where he came from? Can he dribble? Can he score? Can he defend? And so on. The functional competences or peak competences are sometimes easy to measure by simply observing the player during a match. Despite this simple and perhaps obvious fact, candidates in the world of business seldom have their technical skills tested. More often than not, you take their assurances, or their current job title, as proof of their skills and competences, even if the quality of these can vary a lot. The football talent scout cannot be so careless. He must judge and see the player bring home results!

Conclusion

It is necessary to line up clear definitions of the functional as well as social competences so you know what you are looking for. Create a *complete* picture of the prospective recruits' abilities, because only then will you will know if you can develop their talents or not!

- If you are looking for young employees, keep an eye on indirect, descriptive factors that you want to focus on – for example learning, energy, mood and so on. This is crucial when it comes to their ability to develop quickly.
- If you are you looking for experienced employees, then certainly judge their functional competences, but also consider if they are self-motivating, and if they will develop even more. Then you will get a good buy!
- Evaluate the prospect's self-motivation and their ability to handle hardship. Is this done in a constructive or destructive way, not least in relation to the community – the team? Potential clashes may be acceptable as long as they will be solved in a constructive way.

THE SIXTH COMPETENCE
DEVELOP YOUR SECOND-TIER TALENT

The odds that larger football nations such as Brazil, Argentina, France, Germany and Italy will be able to produce big football stars are, statistically speaking, greater than those of smaller football nations such as the Netherlands, Greece and Denmark. This seems logical.

The table on page 94 shows the top 10 national teams as at 26 May 2010 according to FIFA's official ranking of the association's members. FIFA (Fédération Internationale de Football Association) gives points to national teams on a rolling basis according to their international results and the teams played against. The points are gathered as a rolling and weighted average with the latest results having more significance than results obtained a few years ago. FIFA recently changed the somewhat obscure principles and made the ranking simpler, and now the weighting only includes results for the last four years as opposed to eight previously.

From the table you can see that, although some smaller nations are represented, most of the top is dominated by big countries, and this dominance seems prevalent. Smaller nations may drop in and out of the table as the quality of their player's peaks and falls. But overall the picture is clear: big countries have more potentially talented players than small ones!

Although the number of active football players per capita varies, and while there are obviously a number of other factors, it is clear that talented players more often than not come from big football nations that have access to a larger pool of players.

Nonetheless it is interesting to notice that "small football nations" and "small clubs" do win championships – and not just single matches. So let us try to focus on the ability to foster talents and the behind-the-scenes processes of talent development.

	Population (m)	Points	2010	2009	2008	2007	2006
Brazil	190	1611	1	5	2	3	1
Spain	45	1565	2	1	4	7	7
Portugal	11	1249	3	11	11	6	8
Netherlands	16	1231	4	2	10	9	6
Italy	60	1184	5	4	3	1	2
Germany	82	1082	6	3	5	4	9
Argentina	40	1076	7	7	1	5	3
England	51	1068	8	6	9	8	5
France	62	1044	9	10	7	2	4
Croatia	4	1041	10	8	15	11	23

FIFA World rankings: 26 May 2010

The small football nations and clubs have just one chance of withstanding the fierce competition mentioned above, and that is by being more efficient than the big nations when it comes to developing and taking advantage of the talent mass.

Small clubs and nations have to develop and take advantage of the talents available if they want to stand a chance against the competition. Interestingly, this is not unlike the situation many small companies experience in fiercely competitive markets.

So what exactly do these underrated clubs and small football nations do to survive under these highly competitive circumstances? Let us have a look at what the Danish football association DBU (Dansk Boldspil Union) does in order to develop talented players.

Define the development stage of the players

Despite its small size, Denmark (presently ranked 36 according to FIFA) has been over-represented in the final rounds of the major competitions in the last few decades. Although this has only led to one championship, the European Championship of 1992, the performance has been consistent, and it may be helpful to take a look at how the Danish Football Association (DBU) has built a system for player and talent development. Not least because the DBU has found inspiration in both Dutch and English experiences in this area.

The DBU model is based on the premise that training must be adjusted to the age and development stage of the player. The DBU has defined five aspects of training that must be maintained and developed throughout the entire development of the player:

- Technical training
- Tactical training
- Physical training
- Mental training
- Learning environment

DBU's development model

	U5	U6	U7	U8	U9	U10	U11	U12	U13	U14	U15	U16	U17	U18	U19	U20	U21
Technical training Head, body and ball	Basic technical and co-ordination training				Technical skills						Mastering technical skills			Optimising technical skills			
Tactical training Game-awareness	Game play – playing for fun				Team tactics						Team tactics			Team tactics			
Physical training Individual and group	Game play – playing for fun		Jump and sprint		Strength & flexibility				Strength, speed and stamina					Optimising			
Mental training Mental development	Sense of wellbeing				Readiness – visualisation				Goal-setting • motivation • focus • regulating tension						Competitive strategy		
Learning environment Involve and coach	Trainer is engaged and focused on the process				The trainer is involved and challenging						The trainer is demanding			The trainer is aiming to create results			

Within each of the five components, each section or box has its own manual, specifying what kind of training and exercises should be given to each of the age groups. As you might expect, there is a clear difference between the programmes for the younger players (the "hidden jewels") and the older ones (the "young lions").

Throughout the process there is a strong emphasis on the competitive element, both at the individual level and at the team level. This is particularly reflected in the final phase of the "mental training" component – "competitive strategy". The coaching helps players to deal with losing matches, but also, and more importantly, makes them hungry for victory. The players are trained to win.

But training to win is surely not restricted to football teams? How does the business world train to win? Not as effectively, evidently.

The other four components are of course just as important as the "mental training" component, but they are of a more technical character, relating to the game itself. Here, as mentioned in an earlier chapter, the basic skills are trained over and over again until they become almost second nature – whereas in companies, many basic skills are often lost among employees – either forgotten after leaving the school or university, or only sporadically maintained through employment training courses. Another lesson for business leaders to draw from the world of football management.

Develop talent the same way football clubs do!

The DBU, of course, is not a club but a national association which uses the above development model to advise clubs how their training and development should be carried out. In this respect it is perhaps comparable with the Ministry of Education.

But if we draw a parallel to the world of education, we would argue that DBU's development system actually operates on a deeper level than some educational establishments, by showing an even clearer focus on the relationship between development and results.

In the educational sector, schools and colleges across Europe are often accused of concentrating too much on qualifications and too little on development. In addition the delivery of education can become fragmented due to different institutions having inconsistent resources and incoherent goals, not to mention inconsistent grading systems. So it is not only business leaders who can draw inspiration from the world of football, but also educators!

Globalisation and competition – in the world of football and world of business

The DBU model is adhered to strictly throughout Denmark; similar principles are applied in other countries' football communities, albeit in varying shapes and forms. Everywhere, clubs understand that they cannot afford to lose their best performers if they are to compete in the world's most competitive sport. Can we in the world of business draw the same conclusions in a globalised and ever more competitive market?

Remember also that all professional football clubs only train with one goal in mind: winning! In the context of human resources, it is evident that without victory, clubs will be unable to attract talented players, nor will they be able to fund the talents' development (let alone buy in outside players).

In all fairness, there are and will be different views about what is the right "winner strategy" when it comes to developing players. The DBU model is a North European version; other countries, while promoting the same principles, will naturally vary their development systems according to local cultures. But whatever the local variations, businesses can learn one important lesson from the example: without a systematic and conscious approach, from the educational system or the company, players will not get developed – instead, companies will be forced to buy in developed staff on the open market. And you can ask any football team: this is expensive!

Italian club Milan has reached the same conclusion. Milan admits that, unlike Juventus and Inter for example, they have not been good enough at giving their young players match time either on their own squads or by renting them out to other relevant clubs.[29] Milan has been torn between the short-term demand for results – most often achieved by buying in the necessary talent from other teams – and the longer-term choice of recruiting and developing its own talent base from an early age.

Map your dream team, present and future

In the previous chapter we looked at what makes a good talent scout, and what they should be looking for – that is, a combination of both functional and social competences. In the first part of this chapter we have looked at the basic principles of talent development, and considered how the business world can draw inspiration from the world of football management in this crucial area. Let us now get more practical, and consider how these principles can be applied in practice, through the creation of specific tools for managers and business leaders to enable them to create a winning team going for gold!

Many professional clubs, managers and talent scouts start by defining their "dream" team – mapping the layout of the team they would ideally like to assemble. An example is set out below.

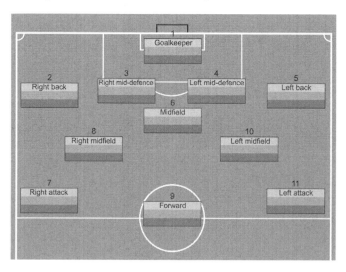

Notice that the pitch is divided into attack, midfield, defence and goalkeepers and may be expanded to include support personnel depending on the size and requirements of the club.

Having determined the types of players required, they then assess whether those players are available among their existing players or whether they have to buy them in from outside, making a note of first second and third choices for each position. They map their existing resources, both current team players and players under development, against the positions identified.

By going through this exercise, the manager and the talent scout can assess the need for recruitment in the short term and medium term, across the whole team. For example, the manager is able to judge whether he lacks striker potential or if his biggest problem is the defence, and so on.

Managers and talent scouts are also able to plot the standard of the players identified, allocating, for example, one, two or three stars according to their level of ability (present and predicted). By doing this, the club is able to put a value on its dream team, both the present and future one.

By using the "dream team" approach, the quantitative evaluation is done according to the manager's favoured playing system, which in the world of business we would translate into strategy, business model, culture and goals.

With this "mapping" available, the manager knows if he has the team that can and will go for gold! And if this is not yet the case, he and the talent scouts have to start looking around again to identify new players in order to build a winning team.

Compare this approach with current practice in the world of business. Although businesses do undoubtedly identify and groom future managers and senior managers from among their ranks, it is rare to adopt the complete "mapping" approach identified above across all levels of an organisation. For example, succession planning will typically only be applied at the very top of an organisation – not at the equally important middle management level. In contrast, the football manager takes into consideration all elements of the team – including defence and midfield – not just the strikers!

What did you overlook? Look at the second tier

Business leaders, like professional football managers, are generally well aware what they want from their staff, but often the in-house talent mass may be inadequate, and the financial resources to recruit externally insufficient. It is true that only the richest clubs in Europe, such as Barcelona, Chelsea and Milan, can afford to buy who they want (subject to availability). These clubs could probably be compared to companies like Microsoft and Coca Cola.

But actually it is exactly when resources are tight that companies can learn from professional football managers. The mapping process described above shows not just the existing talent pool, but also identifies the optimum development path for as-yet undeveloped players.

During our talks with football managers, especially those of smaller clubs, they often point to the fact that you only "borrow" star players, because they are usually quickly sold on to bigger and better clubs such as the ones mentioned above.

And no matter how great a contribution these star players make to the team, it can be difficult to build a stable team if people come and go. In particular, the playing style of the team may be subject to change due to the lack of a solid team foundation.

This does not imply that you should avoid star players. Of course not. But managers of the smaller clubs know that their future will ultimately depend on what they term the "second tier" of talent – players who may not yet be thought of as stars or even as potential stars, but who can be elevated to the benefit of the team, themselves and the continuing quest for gold.

There are many examples of players who have blossomed relatively late in their careers when they received the right level of support and personal development from their team managers. Danish team manager **Morten Olsen** cites the example of former Denmark captain Rene Henriksen[30]. English football legend **Sir**

Stanley Matthews did not win his first major football honours until he was 38 (when he won the FA Cup in 1953).

Some of these second tier players have, as mentioned earlier, developed into national team players without previously having been thought of as potential football stars. This may be the real reason that small clubs and smaller football nations can compete. They have to be – and are – better at taking advantage of the talent mass by deliberately focusing (among other things) on second tier players!

In the world of football you do indeed say that "the bench" wins the cup and the championship, because long and tough competitions will no doubt create hardship and injury among even the biggest stars. In the same way, military tacticians know all too well that it is often the reserves that decide who wins the battle, as Carl von Clausewitz wrote.[31] In fact, von Clausewitz was at Waterloo, where Napoleon was defeated, because the British and Prussians used their reserves in a sensible way.

In the same way, the skilled manager will always look for players in the "second tier" who in the short and long term can make up the core of the team. And here it is appropriate once again to refer to the example of Greece winning the European Championship. A team with no real super stars, but a team which was able to bring home the gold because of the standard of what on a European level would certainly have been considered second tier players!

Few professional football clubs can afford to buy expensive new players *every time* their own stars are sold or injured. Therefore, from a financial perspective, as well as a tactical one, it is doubly important to constantly develop second tier players.

This is done in a very methodical way, focusing on all aspect of the player's profile, including technical skills but also mental and co-operative skills, which we will have a closer look at in the next chapter.

This kind of methodical approach to "team building" is relatively rare in the business world, certainly among smaller companies. Here, the interest in staff development is often more circumstantial and reactive. For example, when an employee leaves or gets sick, managers quickly try to find a suitable replacement – whereas the professional football manager, with the help of his "mapping", already knows who is his first choice, second choice and so on, and whether his players need to be recruited from within own ranks or bought externally.

Development or purchase?

This brings us to a key recruitment issue faced by professional football managers – the choice between internal development and external purchase.

Here, clubs often split into two camps, not unlike companies. Some clubs, for historic reasons, have highly developed youth training facilities and teams which provide a continuing source of potential recruitment to the senior teams. Others have hardly any youth facilities at all.

The latter type of club is, obviously, highly dependent on being able to identify, buy and retain talented players, while large clubs with big youth departments have the privilege of being able to use both options.

Clubs with large talent departments and football academies, however, still need to buy players from other clubs as well. The internal development processes cannot always be relied on to produce the required level of senior players, so most top clubs do in fact reduce their risk and buy in proven talent as well as developing their own home-grown players.

In the business world the choice between internal development and external recruitment is further complicated by the absence of "resale" options for developed staff. This means that the incentive to develop players is arguably smaller than in the world of football, in a purely financial sense. However, the costs of recruitment and the higher salaries demanded by external recruits should tip the scales back in the other direction.

Today, many companies seem to baulk at the prospect of investing substantially in future employees' development and education in return for just a few years of loyalty. However there are obviously many other advantages to businesses in developing existing staff, including operational continuity, confidentiality of products and customer knowledge bases, cultural indoctrination and so on.

It is impossible to say unambiguously whether one model is better than the other. But financially the risks are clearly spread if you have access to both models, and internal staff development is still an area which is largely ignored by far too many business organisations.

Conclusion

- Define the development stages of each of your employees – in each case their development stage should determine the way in which you assess them.
- Define which elements and competences you need to train. These elements depend on the development stage. What stage are your employees at, and which elements do you want to focus on? What are the factors behind your strategy and goals?
- "Map" your team – both your present team and your ideal team – then you will get a clear picture of how your perfect organisation looks. Remember that the "mapping" is based on your preferred – that is, your goals and strategy.
- Rank your key players (present and future) in order of preference in case you cannot get "number one".
- Remember to look at the second tier – surely you have overlooked a talent or two – and they will make up the important core of your organisation, because you only *borrow* stars!

THE SEVENTH COMPETENCE
CREATE GOOD COACHING HABITS

"You can only achieve top performances by working hard. It is not enough simply wanting to win. You have to love both the training session and the match."

"... a good day at work is when the training session (with the team) went well and we had fun. This is actually what I like the very most."
Arsene Wenger, Arsenal[32]

It is natural that a physical sport such as football involves a lot of physical training. But the training is not only physical, and the basis for training today constitutes a highly specialised science which almost every manager follows strictly.

Let us take a look at what kind of managers and assistant managers Italian side Juventus had during 2001-2004.[33]

- *Manager* – directs the matches, selects the team, decides tactics and discusses purchase and sale of players with the rest of the club's executive management.
- *First assistant manager* – often in charge of regular training sessions even though the manager is present. The assistant manager in many cases also acts as advisor and right-hand man to the manager.
- Three *physical trainers* – responsible for creating and supervising the players' physical condition and optimising it.
- One *technical trainer* – one of the three physical trainers is also the "technical" trainer in charge of compiling the training

of technical exercises and tactics for both the individual player and groups of players.

* *Goalkeeper trainer* – as the name implies this speciality trainer has as his sole responsibility to coach the squad's goalkeepers.

Other clubs even employ specialised trainers for defence, midfield and attack, although this was not the case with Juventus at that time (during 2001-2004). Some clubs may also have *several* assistant managers who might be first managers of the important second team, whose players often act as reserves on the first team.

Apart from the above, Juventus's managers utilised a number of support functions:

* Three *physiotherapists* – among them one whose only task was to deal with injuries.
* Two *doctors* – employed full-time.
* Two *masseuses.*
* One *scout* – a "spy" whose job was to monitor opponents during the tournament.

The above shows just how detailed Juventus is in its approach to player management. Other clubs may have one of more of the following specialists involved ad well (competences which Juventus obviously felt were covered by other members of the training staff):

* Dieticians.
* Sport psychologists/mental coaches.

Training is obviously a central part of planning for competition, and within the training function there are several different dimensions and specialisations.

For the sake of the general picture it is worth mentioning that among clubs there is a huge difference as to how the training is carried out. Juventus has emphasised integration of the different disciplines, thereby combining for example the technical training with physical training. By doing this, Juventus has probably stood out and been at the forefront of the development in training principles.

Many business leaders and key persons in organisations and companies do in fact work under pressure and competition similar to what we see in the world of football. Here, too, it is about performing over and over again and coping with competition, both internally in the company and externally in relation to competitors and customers. Exactly the same way as the professional football player and manager must do his utmost at every match in order to achieve victory.

We do believe, though, that many people will agree with us that organisations in the world of business are rarely as systematic or "scientific" in their approach to training for victory as Juventus.

So let us take a closer look at the football training pitch in order to seek inspiration about methodology and principles that enhance the ability to, and the prerequisites for, winning and dealing with competition.

Five basic training principles

The five training principles below are compiled from our general observation of different training regimes that we have encountered. They are outlined and implemented in different ways, and the principles and culture they adhere to vary, but in general we can conclude that professional football managers typically employ the following training components:

- Physical training (and diet)
- Technical training (including tactics)
- Mental training
- Recovery – physically and mentally
- Tournament scheduling and planning

We will now take a closer look at each of the five components, which may have a surprising relevance to the needs of business organisations.

Physical training and diet

Physical training used to be the "mantra" of most training and to a certain degree still is. If only the players were in top shape, things would be fine… If you lacked something technically or tactically, you could always "solve" the problems by using your physique. But with most teams nowadays in good shape, this parameter no longer wins games. At least not on its own. Today, it is regarded as a *minimum* requirement.

During the last 15-20 years, physical training has become much more advanced, both with regard to understanding what the human body is capable of enduring and how best to develop physique to the benefit of the game. Therefore, physical training has undergone a strong tendency to specialisation by using medical science to prepare the training according to the club's desired playing style. Italy has led this trend of using advanced methods to maintain and develop a superior physique. They measure, weigh and test each player both before and during matches to see if his condition is as good as needed.

But even though training and training exercises have evolved over time, the physical basic training still aims at strengthening the following basic player and team elements:

- Condition/endurance
- Speed
- Strength

The players' diet, blood, blood sugar, body fat and so on have also become subject to analysis and recommendations in order to make players perform in the best way at the right time. These principles may vary substantially from club to club, but will certainly be the next area put under control by the club, not least during the important creation of basic physique and the basic training off season and during tournament breaks. As a matter of fact, some clubs already have a diet code or requirements as to what may and should be eaten. Smoking and alcohol have long been banished (almost). When will the world of business be ready to follow suit? When will an active policy on smoking and alcohol be extended with a formal diet policy (advisory, of course)? When will analyses of blood sugar and body mass become requirements? What will the unions say? Is this an inappropriate interference on behalf of the employer, or simply a necessary measure in order to compete in a market economy? We are not sure, but we do believe this will become reality, at least for those going for gold, in the same way that it is already considered natural in the professional football club.

Technical training – including tactical training

Technical training is becoming increasingly common and increasingly detailed in its specialised applications. We will not go into detail regarding these often very advanced and detailed procedures, but simply give a brief overview of the principles behind them.

Players' individual performances are monitored during matches and training so the manager can get back to them later in order to optimise their skills and their playing style. For example, the manager might want to say:

- To the goalkeeper: "You have to practise making fast throw-outs to the right – because this is where we're losing control of the ball."
- To the defender: "You must practise change of play and more 'standard situations', because we are too slow in these areas, the match surveillance shows."
- To the midfielder: "You must practise speed and long passes, because our counter attacks come to a halt because you do not pass on fast enough."
- To the striker: "First time shots at the goal and headers – because this is where you make too many mistakes."

The manager will often look at the squad's overall strengths and deficiencies in relation to the desired playing style as well as the individual players' skills (or lack of them). How much time is spent on this specialised training will vary depending on whether the player is a fixed part of the team and whether the team is currently playing in a tournament. If the team is taking part in a tournament, the training will often be less intensive: more tactics and technique, but less condition training – and the other way around when outside the season. This should and will depend on the individual manager's "school", philosophy and background and not least the team's situation in the present tournament.

As with the "scientification" of the physical training, technical training is becoming more and more detailed as well and subject to quantitative goals. During matches (and sometimes in training) the individual player will have his running, passes and missed passes measured. Based on this assessment, specific individual training schemes aimed at individual players or groups of players are outlined. Strengths are practised and improved; weaknesses are worked on.

Often the greatest difference between clubs is in their specialised technical training, because this training directly supports the manager's desired playing style and tactics. The specialised training may from time to time be the subject of "espionage" among clubs because it – and thus the development of each individual player – is essential to the development of talent and thereby the achievement of success.

Mental training

Mental training has become increasingly important in many clubs. The top clubs' players all have consistently high levels of physical and technical ability. The difference in physical terms between the top teams is marginal. Therefore, most managers will look for new ways that can give their team an advantage. And this is where mental training plays a more and more important role.

Unlike the two previous training elements, there seems to be less consistency when it comes to the use of mental training. Some managers who do not have access to sport psychologists may be wary of using it formally, but will still apply its principles in one form or another.

Often you will see that football players, and other athletes for that matter, develop a little ritual to put themselves into the mood to perform their best. Some teams also develop group rituals, although few football sides take this as far as the All Blacks' famous "haka" performed at the beginning of every New Zealand rugby international.

Among clubs and managers that do *not* use mental coaches, the argument often goes that they are dealing with top motivated players, who through their professional careers have already built up a successful winning mentality. It is interesting, however, that when you ask the top players themselves, several of them believe they could be further optimised through the use of systematic mental training. This differing view on the use of mental training is probably due to the fact that the area is new and still not quite accepted among older managers and training schools.

The mental training is primarily directed at getting the individual player to motivate himself to make the necessary changes to actions, behaviour and attitudes. Usually this is done by having the player visualise successful movements, plays, passes, shots and the like so he can do his best at the right moment. It is during this part of the process the ritual enters the picture.

In reality, controlling the mental state is simply one element of an integrated training process encompassing physical, emotional, mental and spiritual aspects as illustrated in the "high performance

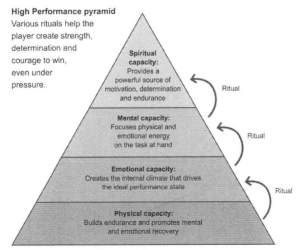

High Performance pyramid
Various rituals help the player create strength, determination and courage to win, even under pressure.

Spiritual capacity:
Provides a powerful source of motivation, determination and endurance

Ritual

Mental capacity:
Focuses physical and emotional energy on the task at hand

Ritual

Emotional capacity:
Creates the internal climate that drives the ideal performance state

Ritual

Physical capacity:
Builds endurance and promotes mental and emotional recovery

After Jim Loehr and Tony Schwartz: "The Making of a Corporate Athlete",
Harvard Business Review January 2001, p. 123.

pyramid" below.

As the pyramid shows, the foundation for the development of mental and spiritual strength is the player's physical capacity. Having established a physical base, the player must develop emotional strength, learning, amongst other things, to control his emotions on the pitch. From this point the player can develop his mental focus, and thereafter his spiritual capacity providing a powerful source for ongoing motivation and endurance.

Certainly the player must be in good physical shape, but he must also be in a "high energy state" mentally in order to perform 100 percent.

The mental training aims to make the player able to control his mental state, so that he can create the "ideal performance state" to bring home results. This requires careful training. Most football managers adopt the same routines, procedures or "rituals" for both training and matches, allowing a consistent "rhythm" to be developed on and off the pitch.

It is interesting to watch well-balanced and successful top teams training. The atmosphere is relaxed, even cosy sometimes, but still fully concentrated. There are many exercises with fixed rhythms and recurring elements. The teams will continue training when they play tournaments and between matches. Not heavily, but simply to maintain the rhythm of the squad – and the training then becomes almost ritual (although of course also physical). These rituals are designed to put individual players and the team as a whole in a positive state of mind.

Compare this approach to the modern company with its fragmented and *ad hoc* approach to employee motivation. The daily life of many organisations and employees is filled with incoherent and stressed workflows, but employees are not helped mentally to deal with these. No attempt is made to provide consistency, but rather to find changes in an endless quest for optimisation. Perhaps a ritual or two could provide the necessary karma, as in the world of football – rituals capable of providing the necessary rhythm to allow the generation of innovation and optimisation. Any manager or football player knows that the key is to "find the rhythm". Being able to understand and find the work rhythm can be facilitated by, among other things, the use of relevant and motivating rituals.

The pyramid's final level is the spiritual level – in effect, the source of self-esteem and positive self-image. Whereas the lower levels of the pyramid can be influenced – and sometimes controlled, manipulated and stimulated by – external factors such as physical exercises, diet and training exercises, the spiritual level is not that easy to access.

In many respects this is an effort of will on the player's part. Players (or employees) must regard training exercises as a means to create the foundation for a positive self-image that ensures the necessary self-belief. This belief brings with it the will, courage and endurance needed to perform optimally. To put it simply, the employer (or, in the football, context, the club) can deliver the means to achieve the three lowest levels, but the employee (or player) must himself maintain or change his self-perception on the upper level in order to achieve success – and often this is what distinguishes the "star players" from other good players. Despite the circumstances, star players often have an immense belief in themselves and their potential, which creates positive and winning situations, whereas ordinary players often begin to lose confidence when they encounter difficulties. The skilled mental coach and the skilled manager respectively will be keenly aware of this when dealing and communicating with players or employees.

Arsenal's **Arsene Wenger** is a good example of a football manager who works hard on the lower levels of the pyramid by using a systematic and scientific approach to physical training. But it is through his interaction with his top players – and the respect he shows them – that he gives the players the confidence to take their performance to the next level. Arsene Wenger is known to show great respect for his players, although nobody is in doubt who is in charge and who selects the team. Wenger seems – consciously or unconsciously – to stimulate the egos of the top players and hence their self-image – the final level of the performance pyramid.

How many business leaders can claim to do the same with their employees? How many employees feel like better human beings when they return home from work? Only those who have a clever and skilful leader!

Recovery – physical and mental

Most people know that following a top performance, you need to recover both physically and mentally. And in this area, we all have much to learn from the world of football – because as a matter of fact most football players spend quite a lot of time doing nothing. They are recovering!

The span of the recovery period depends on whether the team is taking part in a tournament or not. Outside the season the training is often focused on physical elements in order to improve condition and strength as well as systems and tactics during training matches. During the season the training becomes more technical and tactical and only moderately physical. Obviously, this is because the body needs to recover before the next match later in the week. So it is not a good thing to train too heavily, because you will become over-trained, perform less well and risk injury.

Studies into exhaustion show, perhaps predictably, that players "sprint" less the more matches they play in a short time.[34] They run the same distance, but the result is an inferior peak performance. Only time for recovery can solve this issue.

The same goes for mental build-up. As we saw with mental training, half the performance lies in retaining the energy for the match day, those 2x45 minutes. Everything else is simply preparation.

In a similar way you might speak of build-up and recovery during a day, a week, a month, the year and so on. In fact, studies show that the human body and brain is geared towards performances during certain periods. We need a break every 90-120 minutes – which happens to be the time a football match takes![35] The world of football has understood this for a long time, so their training sessions usually last about 120 minutes in the morning and 60-120 minutes in the afternoon.

What about us in the business world? We work overtime and intensively for 2x4-5 hours – maybe just cut into two by a frantic lunch break! Often we work evenings and weekends as well. Our claim, which studies from the world of sport support, is that the value and performance during the last hours are very marginal. The world of football knows this. So remember to recover if you want to give a top performance.

Team and tournament training and planning – understand when you must perform your best

In the same way that a day and a week in the world of football have their cycles, so does the year. And as we recognise from other sports, in football too the goal is to build up the team's optimal strength so players can reach their peak at the time when the important games are played (for example at the top or bottom of the league). Certain teams are expected to be weak during spring, but they train in order to peak during the fall and so on – sometimes depending on the tournament schedule (and the opponents), and also taking into account anticipated gains and losses of players.

In any case, the planning for the year is much more rigorous than we see in the business world, which rarely takes into full consideration the times when their organisation should reach peak performance. The world of football knows very well that after a match comes recovery, both mentally and physically. But this is the case with companies as well, and yet when it comes to this, companies – particularly knowledge-based ones – work far too intensively for a prolonged time, often encouraging extended overtime. The truth is that it requires a long-term, planned approach to achieve peak performances when they are required. So if your organisation has a lot of overtime, you must and should – like the football club – plan when the organisation needs to recover. Is it during spring, next month or next week? This may, of course, vary depending on the size of the organisation. But if you do not plan it, you will accomplish mediocre results.

It is a well-known fact from the world of football that big teams with their often large squads are resistant to injury and pressure on key players and also better at dealing with both local and international tournaments – including lending players to national teams.

But your organisation is hardly any different from the football team. Periods with a lot of pressure must and should be followed by periods with less pressure.

Create your own training principles – learn from football

The above illustrates the basic principles that typically apply to a professional football club's training during the day, the week, the month and the year. It seems clear and easy to understand when talking about a football team. But how can we apply these principles to the workplace?

Using football's five training principles as the point of departure, below we will come up with some suggestions as to how they can be incorporated into modern organisations.

Physical training (and diet)

Make an agreement with the employees to work out, focusing on both condition and strength. The company may be willing to pay for this in the form of a gym or sports club membership, for example. You could consider sharing training costs (and time) agreeing that half the training takes place within working hours and the other half outside, considering that the "prize" benefits both parties. Employees in great shape work harder, longer and more efficiently besides thinking and solving tasks faster and better!

Diet is another element, increasingly recognised by companies. Many companies today provide canteens or subsidised lunch facilities with a focus on healthy eating. And perhaps in the future we will see companies only hiring "healthy" employees in the same way that smokers are not welcome in many places today.

Technical speciality training – maintain strengths and train weaknesses

Put into system the technical training for you and your employees. This could be performance skills, or it may be IT or languages. But first of all look at it in relation to the role or future role of the employee and the company's strategy. A defender should not be a striker, and a striker should not be a defender. Do as the manager does – take notes, so you can tell both yourself and your colleagues where they need further training. And remember to maintain your strengths – these are often the ones winning the matches!

Mental training – create the basis for improved self-esteem and show respect towards your colleagues and employees

If you are not fully aware about how to encourage either yourself or your employees, incorporate rituals that may be visible or invisible. An example: every time you attend an in-house meeting, perform a set of actions that put you or your colleagues in a positive mood. And remember that praise and obvious respect is a "must", and essential to ensure a positive response to any possible future criticism, because employees are like football players – they tend to want to fulfil your expectations if you respect them.

Recovery – physical and mental – plan the day, the week and the month

Be careful with planning. You might want to plan only 50-60 percent of your day – otherwise the energy will disappear and overtime will close in. The same goes for the week. Make sure to recover in your spare time and during the weekend. When do you plan on recovering physically and mentally, and how? The truth is that our lives nowadays are hectic and that we often forget to recover.

Team and tournament planning – plan the year

During which parts of the year do you and your organisation peak? Plan your holiday. Do not postpone it until the last moment as so many other people do. You need to use your holiday to recover. Plan in the same way over the span of a year.

And above all, learn to make the most of training, for yourself as well as for your employees – both physically and intellectually.

Conclusion

- Define your own and your colleagues' physical training and, if possible, create a fixed diet. And stick to it – if you take it seriously, so will your employees and colleagues.
- Work on your weaknesses and become better. Also train to your strengths. Be specific as in the world of football and become your own specialist trainer, or ask for feedback to your training. Do it after each match (situation), but not by uninspiring development talk – coaching takes place right here on the pitch right now!
- Develop ritual behaviours that promote positive mental energy – your physical energy is the basis for this.
- Recover – physically and mentally. Remember to include breaks during the day, the 24 hours, the week and the year. Keep them and understand your cycles or you will over train and risk making mistakes (and injury).
- Team and tournament training (planning): Define during which periods you and your organisation need to perform most. When do you need to be "on a roll" and when are you more or less dependent on top performance?

THE EIGHTH COMPETENCE
EMPOWER PROBLEM-SOLVERS

A certain player on the Danish national team (whose name we have promised not to disclose) was not always considered to be national team potential. During his youth he lacked a belief in his own talent and did not, to put it bluntly, show very much ambition during training and matches. In his own mind, he saw himself playing at a much lower level than his potential warranted. A true talent would have been wasted had it not been for managers who knew how to coach him, thereby enabling him to achieve much more than he himself had imagined. By being coached by different managers, he realised that he did indeed have what was needed to make it in the big European leagues. And this is exactly where he finds himself today.

Top manager **José Mourinho** sees training as a totally natural tool when developing his players and the team. Not just personal coaching, but team coaching as well. As an example, Mourinho will time and again stop his players in the middle of an exercise he himself set up and ask them if it could be improved. By doing this, he makes his players think the training through. This makes them more aware of the process and ensures that the training becomes deeply anchored. At the same time, he uses his players' competences to improve the training even more and thereby their skills and competences.

The essence of both examples is the same: with coaching, managers have raised the bar and taken maximum advantage of the players' potential.

When was the last time you coached your employees?

What is coaching?

The role of the business leader changes all the time and this applies more than ever in the present economic climate. If we look at the changes our world is undergoing, it is quite natural that we as leaders need to change our actions as well.

The role of the manager before and now

Before	Now
Manage employees	Develop and recruit employees
Authority by title	Authority by personality
Administer technology	Develop technology
National competition	International competition
Huge entrance barriers	Blurring of sector barriers
Demand for the use of fewer raw materials	Ultimate demand for the use of fewer raw materials
Employees work for management	Employees work with management
Hierarchical organisations	Flat organisations

The demand for improved performance using fewer resources is a mantra that is constantly repeated by managers. The solution is to get more out of the resources you already have. This means you need to develop your employees' competence profile. The good news is that your employees are probably capable of much more than they themselves think. The challenge is "just" making them realise it. And the tool here is coaching.

Coaching is a tool that the world of sport used long before the business world, and it is still in this world that it is most widely used.

The recognition that we as individuals are capable of much more when we are challenged and helped along is more evident in the world of sports.

The football manager is very aware that he is 100 percent dependent on the players. They – and only they – decide his production capital. Unlike the people in charge in the world of business, he cannot put his faith in a unique product, a cheaper price or own distribution just to name a few. The players are his 11 "starters" who will execute his strategy.

There are many definitions of coaching. One of the grand old men of coaching, Tim Gallwey, describes it this way: "Coaching means unlocking a person's potential in order for them to maximise their own performance. It means helping people to learn instead of teaching them."[36]

In his book *The Manager as Coach and Mentor*, Eric Parloe puts it even more bluntly, defining coaching as "a structured, mutual process where people develop skills and achieve precise competences through evaluations, guided real-life experiences and regular feedback."[37]

Top manager **José Mourinho**'s version of coaching is coined "guided discovery". He believes that players on a team at this level will not accept being spoken to in a non-involving way. When he needs to develop them, the player has to contribute considerably himself – backed up, of course, by Mourinho.

Our own definition of coaching is: "Coaching is a management tool which, by using directed questions and open conversations, makes the person being coached open up his resources and operational options and thereby makes him capable of solving the challenge in question."

In other words, coaching is the tool you should use when you enhance the coached person's performance using *conversation*. Not by telling the person being coached what he should do, but rather by asking questions that enable him to come up with the solutions himself.

After Peter Hansen-Skovmoes and Gert Rosenkvist: "Coaching as a Tool for Development" in Reinhard Stelter: *Coaching – Learning and Development,* Psykologisk Forlag, 2002

The different kinds of conversation can be adapted according to individual circumstances. However, as a general rule we believe that coaching should be done in an environment as power-free as possible, and *questions* should be the coach's main tool.

It is not essential to define exactly what the coach can or cannot say. It *is* essential, however, that he is able to pose questions and keep his own opinions out of the conversation. The focal point is the development of the person being coached.

Advantages of coaching

Coaching can be used in many ways to develop your employees – to facilitate problem-solving, improve motivation, develop team behaviours, and so on. The advantages are plenty, to the individual concerned, to the manager, and to the organisation as a whole:

To the employee

- Greater motivation, self confidence and competence. Who does not want to experience finding the solution to a problem themselves? This is exactly the experience you get when you solve a challenge by the use of coaching.
- Relaxation of deadlocked situations.
- Remove barriers that make it impossible for the person being coached to learn and develop.
- Closer relationship with the coach, as the coaching process bring the two closer together.

To the business leader

- You will free up some much needed time! In a paced and busy world you will find that your employees can take on more and more responsibility. Simply because you coached them and thus developed their skills and competences further.
- Better usage of the resources your employees represent.
- Your own skills are developed, and your department/division becomes a more attractive place to work.

To the company

- More skilled employees, better results, greater efficiency, better work environment and so on. And it is absolutely free!

Do you see the advantages?

According to a study conducted in Denmark, companies can potentially add 30 percent to their value by using coaching! The same study shows that only four in ten employees are happy about their immediate manager's effort to bring out the best in them. Although the authors of the study do stand to benefit from promoting the advantages of coaching, there is no doubt about its potential.[38]

A ten-minute review of the coaching process

There is no single correct way to coach, and it is beyond the reach of this book to present an in-depth introduction to the methodology of coaching. The following does, however, give a fair summary of the basic procedure:

1   Create agreement about the subject.
    • Sounds obvious, but ensures you stay focused on the relevant topic and are not disturbed by other things.
    • Pose questions such as: "What is the most important thing you want to talk about?"

2   Decide on the desired goals.
    • Make sure you know when you have reached the agreed goal.
    • Pose questions such as: "What is the purpose of us talking about x?" and "What would you like to achieve?"

3   Create understanding/give new perspectives.
    • The person being coached needs to fully understand the area the coaching process deals with. This makes different solutions become clear.
    • Pose questions such as: "How do you view this problem?" and "What does this mean in reality?"

4   Determine the problem-solving process.
    • Who should do what and when?

5   Create room for manoeuvre.
    • Pose questions such as: "What specifically are you going to do?" and "How do you view the 'path' you need to follow?"
    • Pose questions such as: "Do you have the necessary resources?" and "Do you need support?"

6   Sum up.
    • Pose questions such as: "What are your biggest challenges?"

The figure shows that if the employee's qualifications are low, the natural management tool to use is instructive or authoritarian behaviour. In these cases the manager controls the performance of the task. The more qualified the employee is, the less the need for the manager's active supervision.

Finding out which of the four management styles is the ideal depends, among other things, on the need to be controlling or supporting.

Ricardo Izecson dos Santos Leite (better known as Kaka) is one of the world's best playmakers. Kaka is a star on both the Brazilian national team and at one of Europe's best clubs, Milan Real Madrid. Before joining Madrid he played for Milan. The club's manager at that time, **Carlo Ancelotti**, said: *"Before a match I don't tell Kaka where to play. He can figure that out himself. He decides whether to stand 10 metres further in front or behind. He follows his instinct, and I am fine with that."*[41] Ancelotti's management style with Kaka based on delegation. He knows that before the start of a match, a player such as Kaka does not need a lot of instructions. He simply works better when given a substantial amount of freedom.

During the 2000 European Championships, Steven Gerrard enters the pitch. England is in front 1-0 and needs to win the match. Manager at the time **Kevin Keegan** uses instructive management when he says: "Just play the way you usually do for Liverpool. Make sure we have the ball. Stop the German attacks, because they are close to breaking through our barriers. And Steven, enjoy the game!"[42]

In this situation, it is not possible for Keegan to give a long explanation (which he has probably done before the match started), and he therefore chooses to give Gerrard a short instruction.

The point here is that one management style is not superior to another. It depends 100 percent on the situation.

In order for a business leader to be able to use situational management, he or she needs to have three skills:

- The manager needs to view/evaluate the situation and the employee's level of development.

- He needs to be able to shift between the different management styles.
- He needs to build a bridge to the employee so they get a common understanding of the level the employee is presently at.

By using these three skills you can choose which kind of management style is best suited to the situation. Be very conscious about this. The same person can easily be in need of different kinds of management depending on the situation.

Coaching and the football manager

John Whitmore writes in his book *Coaching on the Job*: "Coaching is not just a technique brought out and used strictly during certain specific circumstances. It is a way to manage, a way in which to treat people, a way of thinking, a way of being."[43]

The world of football has many good coaches to whom coaching is an integrated part of their management style. **José Mourinho** is one of them. One of the clearest examples is his coaching of technically strong midfielder Joe Cole.

Cole had been bought by Mourinho's predecessor, **Claudio Ranieri**, for seven million pounds, but he never managed to secure a fixed spot in the team despite his obvious skills and potential. This is primarily because he was not seen as a team player. During a game against Liverpool, Cole scored the only goal of the match. Yet Mourinho said afterwards: *"After he scored, the game finished for Joe. I need eleven players for defensive organisation and I had just ten."*[44]

Eventually, Cole's understanding of the game opened up, and he began to show his true character. His failure to understand that he played as part of a team was gone. Cole says about Mourinho: *"He was the first manager to look at me and my game in a serious way. He has had an enormous influence on my career. I listen to him – he is among the best in Europe."*[45]

Another example of a player who has learned from Mourinho's coaching skills is Deco: *"Mourinho is unique, because he is capable of changing the way a player thinks. He didn't change my playing style – he improved it. He made me think much more about what I do."*[46]

Mourinho is a great example of football coaching at its best, enabling his players to find their true potential both as individuals and as team players. Imaging what you would achieve if you could offer your own staff and employees the same opportunities.

Coaching and the leader

Not everyone goes to work just because they get paid to. We also show up because we feel the job is allowing us to develop, because we are taken seriously, because feel that we make a difference. This is the reason why coaching is and should be the most important management tool available to us. Coaching is specifically based on the needs of each employee, based on his particular development stage and his individual motivational needs. Coaching is the key to ensuring a fully motivated workforce, working to the maximum of their ability.

Only 44 percent of respondents in the Danish study referred to above said that they were "very satisfied" or "satisfied" with their immediate superior's effort to trigger the full potential in them. Try figuring out how many of *your* organisation's employees are satisfied. You may find it is fewer than you expect. This could represent a huge untapped resource, waiting to be released by an effective coaching programme.

But why do employees have these needs, and what is it exactly that motivates them? Are they not satisfied as long as we tell them what to do and how to do it? Why do they wish to get developed? American psychiatrist Frederick Herzberg has part of the explanation.

Motivation theory

According to Herzberg, people are influenced by two types of factors in their workplace, which he defined as "hygiene factors" and "motivation factors":[47]

Hygiene factors	Motivation factors
• Pay and benefits • Company policy & administration • Relationships with co-workers • Supervision • Status • Job security • Working conditions	• Achievement • Recognition • The work itself • Responsibility • Advancement • Growth

Hygiene factors are extrinsic factors – they do not lead to higher motivation but dissatisfaction exists without them. Motivation factors are intrinsic – they lead to job satisfaction and higher levels of motivation.

Business coaching is directed primarily at the motivational factors. It is designed to increase satisfaction and motivation, and help employees meet their need for self-esteem and self-realisation, as Maslow would have put it. By enabling individuals to find their own solutions, the individuals are empowered, and their self-esteem reinforced.

Conclusion

We do not take full advantage of our employees' resources simply because we do not help them along! Coaching is a unique tool to expand your employees' resources and at the same time make sure that you get more time available in your capacity as a leader.

Get inspired by the following and secure an advantage:

- Pose questions so the person being coached can come up with answers himself. You should not provide the answers.
- Keep focused on the development of the person being coached.
- Use models such as GROW as the basis of your own coaching style.
- You create greater competence and better results for your organisation – and it doesn't cost you anything.
- It expands your own competence as a manager considerably.
- You will be known as the boss who develops his employees.
- Remember that coaching is not rocket science.
- The more you coach your employees, the longer they will stay with you. Think about how much recruitment money you will save.

How many of your employees are capable of much more than they think? Find out today.

THE NINTH COMPETENCE
KNOW YOUR COMPETITOR

In 2007, **Sven-Goran Eriksson** took charge of Premier League club Manchester City. Previously, he had been manager of clubs such as Benfica, Roma, Fiorentina, Sampdoria and Lazio as well as the English national team. This was obviously an auspicious moment for Manchester City.

And indeed it did not take long before changes began to be seen at the club. For example, the following job ad was posted in late 2007:

Manchester City Performance Analyst Role

As part of the re-launch of our analysis team, three new positions will be created:

Opposition analyst: As an individual with a high level of game understanding and a talent for communicating clear and effective messages, you will profile our opposition by collaborating both our objective and subjective analysis. Working alongside our coaching staff and players, you will facilitate creation of 'game plans', using your innovation and knowledge of best practice to maximise the delivery of key information. The successful candidate will have at least 2 years experience in preparing teams for competition in elite sport, must hold a UEFA B licence or equivalent, and must have experience working with match analysis and video editing software ...

Source: www.pzfootball.co.uk 29 January 2008.

Sven-Goran Eriksson is totally convinced that the more you know about your competitor, the bigger your chance of winning. Only through analysis and planning of different scenarios can you anticipate what will happen tomorrow.

How many of your company's employees have this task as their main job?

You win when you know your competitor

With the right knowledge about your opponents or competitors at hand, you can plan the initiatives needed in order for your team or company to reach the goals you have laid out. If you can answer questions such as: "What is the opponent's play system or strategy like?", "What are his strong and weak points?", "How can we put him under pressure?" and "What will their reaction be?", then you are able to plan and prepare your resources. In short, by coming up with a picture of your competitors' reaction profile you can create your strategy.

A strategy:

- determines the direction you want to follow.
- focuses your efforts on what you think is important in order to reach your goals.
- defines what your organisation is.
- ensures consistency.

(inspired by "Strategy safari" by Mintzberg, Ahlstrand and Lampel)

It is obvious that knowledge about your competitors plays an important role when working out your strategy, and this has indeed always had a prominent place among business leaders and in management literature.

As an example, the business strategists of the 1980s were deeply inspired by military history and literary classics such as von Clausewitz's *On War* (1812)[48] and Sun Tzu's *The Art of War* (approx. 320 b.c.). Both became "must reads" in large parts of the business world and still are today.

Sun Tzu wrote: "In general, whoever first arrives at the battlefield and can await the arrival of the enemy is relaxed, while the party that arrives later and has to launch an attack is exhausted." This is a remark most business people and football players know all too well. Von Clausewitz writes that strategy is based in a world that changes all the time. Therefore strategy should have a flexible foundation. Anyone who has seen or played even a few football games will recognise this.

One of the most popular books about marketing is Al Ries and Jack Trout's *Marketing Warfare*. In the book, many lessons learned from famous battles throughout history are used in reference to the world of business. The authors note, among other things, that if one side in a contest wants to win, it must "focus its efforts on outwitting, outmanoeuvring or outnumbering the opponent."[49] Here as well, the analogy to the world of football is evident.

The basis of any strategy is, as described above, knowledge about the market. In the world of business this means gathering information about customers, trends in society, economic and political factors, sales channels, the competition's strengths and weaknesses, and so on. This task seems simple, but few companies collect this kind of knowledge in a systematic way. In this area, the world of business is reactive, and much of the information gathered about opponents' activities is obtained more or less by chance – more often than not by the sales force. The problem is that this is a random rather than a systematic gathering of vital information.

In the world of football, on the other hand, the analytical work is concentrated on fewer issues, but is more in-depth than in the world of business – and nothing is accidental.

What do football managers do?

It is quite obvious that football managers try to know as much as possible about their next opponent. Does the opposite side prefer playing 4:3:3, 4:4:2, 1:4:2:3 or maybe 5:3:2? Or perhaps variants of these formations? Are they focused on technique or is it pure muscle power that they rely on? Do they have a defensive or offensive midfield? Are they dangerous during set-piece situations? Do their wings create most of their chances? Is their defence aggressive? Do they rely on counter-attacks? Or is their play focused on "total football"?

The answers to these questions and many, many more are gold-dust to all football mangers when they need to select the team and tell the players what strategy to use during the particular match.

Manchester City's job ad shows that this is a club that fully supports these principles. Sven-Goran Eriksson and his team realise that the more they know about the opponent, the less they will be taken by surprise during the match. Because they are prepared!

This disciplined approach is common in the football world, as we have discovered during all the research we have done preparing this book.

In 2004, Porto played Monaco in the Champions League final. Porto Manager **José Mourinho** was well prepared:

"We began preparations for this match by all of us watching a lot of our opponent's matches on video. I already knew what was worth knowing about Monaco's team, but I wanted the players to know as much as I did. I wanted them to see for themselves just how fast Giuly was when he launched a counter-attack; how Morientes, the goal scorer, was always on the spot at the right time; how calm Rothen was when leading an attack; and in general how Monaco's team moved around on the pitch when both attacking and defending. Apart from gaining this general knowledge we also did something we had never done before. Each of our players was handed a DVD which he had to watch and analyse. For example, Paula Frerreia got a DVD showing how his counterpart on Monaco's team, winger Rothen, played both along with his team mates and alone. Our central defender got a similar DVD showing how Morientes and Prsos played. Each player received his own DVD to study. After everyone had watched their DVD we had a joint discussion about what each of us had observed. In this way we got to know the Monaco team, and I do not think the French side had any secrets left that we did not know."[50]

Porto won the match 3-0.

Football managers all over the world, in large and small clubs, use enormous amounts of time looking into the opponents' strengths and weaknesses. There is, however, a huge variation in the tools big and small clubs have access to in order to conduct this surveillance.

Low technology aids

Little information is better than no information. This is what football managers of teams in the lower leagues have to realise. They manage clubs that cannot afford to send them around the country to observe their upcoming opponents. And they have the disadvantage that the football matches broadcast on TV only involve teams from the best league. Press coverage of the lower league they take part in is also negligible.

But that does not make them give up. Either they themselves go to the competitors' stadiums and observe future opponents to figure out how they play, what systems they prefer, and which good players need to be followed closely. Or they may give their contacts a call asking for their analysis of the upcoming opponent. This might be a sports journalist from a local paper providing them knowledge about a new striker or defender worth knowing about. Or it could be one of the manager's own men who previously has played for the opponents and therefore knows which players are excellent headers of the ball or who needs it at his feet in order to be a threat. And whether the defenders are fast or slow, or if the team will only last three quarters of the game.

Even great managers such as **José Mourinho** use low technology aids. During one deciding match where Porto met Benfica in order to qualify for the UEFA Cup, he simply dispatched a spy to observe Benfica's training sessions. The spy watched the training and spoke with other people about the club and then made the assessment that dangerous striker Jankauskas would be on the pitch from the first whistle. With this knowledge, Mourinho had plenty of time to prepare his strategy and instruct his players how to keep Jankauskas out of the game. Mourinho's team won, and Jankauskas did not score a single goal.[51]

The more fortunate managers are able to use TV to monitor their teams' performance. They can study the match, take notes of main events and afterwards show their players, on the screen, what they need to focus on. Other managers get their assistant managers or other confident employees to do the analyses.

High technology aids

Manchester United plays in one of the world's best and toughest football leagues. Besides Premier League and FA Cup matches, there are also Champions League matches to take part in. This requires an extremely professional method of analysis in order to assess the opponents' strengths and weaknesses. **Sir Alex Ferguson**, for example, likes to use high technology aids:

> *"I use different forms of IT equipment because it provides me with all the information I need. Back before, you used to take a lot of notes, but I have never really managed to read them out loud during team meetings or give them to players. But nowadays we in Manchester United have become really good at doing video analyses. We have two men employed full-time to take care of this. Because, as with so many other things in life, technological development has reached this area as well. And the latest addition to the range of tools that enable us to observe the opposition is ProZone..."[52]*

ProZone was first revealed in 1998, and managers such as Sir Alex Ferguson, Arsene Wenger, Steve McClaren and Sven-Goran Eriksson rely heavily on it.

It is a surveillance and statistics system that utilises computer technology and 16 cameras to monitor how each player performs. For example, the user will get detailed information about how long a distance each player runs, how fast and high he jumps, how many perfect passes he makes, how quickly he is in position during a set-piece situation and much more. All of it precious information that tells the manager where the opponent is strong and where he is weak.

The ProZone system, obviously, also has the advantage that the manager can assess his own team's potential for improvement. Imagine just how useful the following knowledge given to Sir Alex Ferguson must have been to him:

The ProZone system monitored Manchester United's Wayne Rooney during the 2004/2005 season. Among other things, the information gathered showed that he would go an average distance of 11.82 kilometres per match. Four of these kilometres he would run, 4.8 kilometres would be done at jogging speed, one kilometre at a light sprint and 500 metres at a full sprint. He touched the ball 105 times during a game – 90 times with his feet, 13 times with his chest and twice with his head.[53]

Using this intelligence, Ferguson could expand his own knowledge and ideas of how to make Rooney an even better player.

How is this knowledge passed on to the players?

The way in which managers choose to pass on their knowledge about the opponents to their own players differs a lot. Some prefer to hold a small briefing about the opposite side just before the match, and by doing this they focus on their own team's playing style. Others will brief the team and the individual players before the showdown and will refer to this briefing during the next training session.

During the qualification to the 2008 European Championship, Denmark faced Spain in two extremely important matches. Besides being Denmark's "recurring nightmare" when it comes to football, Spain has an exceptionally good team. In order to try to change this imbalance, assistant manager **Peter Bonde** went to great lengths to analyse the Spanish team's strengths and weaknesses. Among the results were a good understanding of which 11 players Spain were likely to use – and Bonde was able to plan his own team using this information.

The analysis was divided into two parts:

- Spain's team tactics and set-piece situations.
- Individual player observation.

"This is the match I have spent most time researching. During the weeks before the match I spent a lot of time using the video analysis programme. Using this, we could give the players a thorough briefing about the Spanish team's strengths and weaknesses. Both as a team and individually. I had gathered 150-170 sequences from Spain's last few matches and passed on the most important information to the players."[54]

Denmark had a great match for the first 20 minutes, right up to the point that left fielder Niclas Jensen was red-carded! In the end they lost 2-1.

Former Liverpool manager **Rafael Benitez** likes to get a video presentation of the upcoming opponents focusing on the most important details of their play. The presentation does not take more than an hour. Before the memorable Champions League final against Milan in 2005, Benitez concluded: *"They get worn out, and during second half they are significantly weaker, so we can launch an attack against their central defence if we know how to use our strengths."[55]*

After the first half, Liverpool trailed by three goals. During seven minutes of the second half, they scored three times and won the Champions League cup after extra time and a penalty shoot-out.

To what extent do we do it in the business world?

The business leader is responsible for continuously monitoring changes in the business environment. Most companies invest a lot of resources monitoring their production efficiency, the prices of raw materials, interest and currency rates and other operational variables. But these do not provide management with the overview needed to push the organisation in the right direction. That can only come by keeping an eye on the competition's products and their plans to launch new products or campaigns, by analysing trends in demand, assessing the impact of technological developments on distribution, and so on.

Although many companies do consider these issues sporadically, few do it systematically. Certainly, it is still rare for companies have a department in charge of analysis or working systematically with competitor surveillance.

So the conclusion is clear. Once again, we can learn a lot from the world of football.

How do we do it in the business world?

In the data-rich 21st century it is hardly information that companies lack. We are able to get easy access to figures and analysis on everything from customer preferences, the value of our brands, competitors' investment in commercials, our closest rivals' financial results, which companies have what patents and the like. The challenge is rather how to organise and take advantage of this information.

The answer is: *by using a Marketing Information System (MIS).* The MIS system is defined as: "A structure that, through continuous interplay, collects, sorts, analyses, evaluates and distributes current and precise information needed to make decisions that improve the planning, implementation and guidance of marketing."[56]

In other words a system that ensures relevant information as a basis for the decisions that the people in charge of management need to make. "Marketing is too important to leave it to the marketing department," someone once said. It is indeed true that this information system is not only intended for the marketing management. The MIS should be the place where the whole organisation gets its information about the marketplace in which it operates.

The system may come in different shapes and forms. This is how Philip Kotler imagines it:

Marketing Information System (MIS).

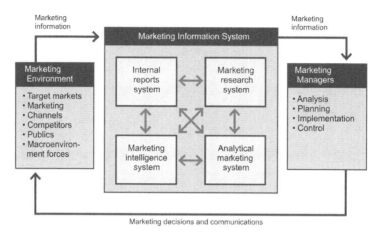

Source: Philip Kotler, *Marketing Management*
Pearson Education, 2002.

- *Internal reports system* – the data that is already available in the company's internal systems. For example sales reports, customer lifestyle preferences, stocks, orders, product costings, customers' purchase history and so on.
- *Marketing intelligence system* – data about relevant developments within the organisation's environment. Imagine how much information your salespeople and distributors can provide you. "Mystery shoppers" is another relevant option.
- *Marketing research system* – this deals with the market analysis an organisation needs and which are not covered by the above two points. It could be a survey of how consumers view a new product (pre-launch) and the like.
- *Analytical marketing system* – is made up of a statistical bank and a model bank. The former is a collection of statistical procedures to extract relevant information from data. The model bank is a compilation of models that makes the organisation capable of extracting relevant knowledge from data.

What are the similarities between the above and the football manager's analytical work? A first sight, not many! Othmar Hitzfeld, Fabio Capello and Bernd Schuster hardly spend time studying macro economic factors when they judge their upcoming opponents! But the whole point is that they have actually built up a system that to a high degree resembles Philip Kotler's MIS. Their "internal report system" is the measurement that team doctors and physical managers use to evaluate and measure the players. The manager's "marketing intelligence system" is the information he gets from his own players, former players he has coached and other informal sources. The "marketing research system" is the system used when Real Madrid's assistant manager travels to Allianz Arena to see for himself what shape Bayern Munich's troops are in before their Champions League showdown. Finally, the "analytical marketing system" is the system Manchester United's "spies" use when analysing Arsenal's latest game before their match meeting next weekend.

This is how we should do it

The world of football is good at focusing on the recent past. That is, football managers concentrate on the last few matches and analyse trends in physical condition, play systems (strategy), results and so on. The surveillance methods are extensive and "close up" – enabling direct study of individual (and team) strengths and weaknesses.

Conclusion

In the world of business, companies *do* commission and utilise market reports. But only a few companies do it continuously, and more than once a year. Most do it less often! Imagine if companies monitored their competitors as skilfully as football managers do. Think about the impact it would have on our strategic work and ability to beat the competition.

Find inspiration in the below and grab an advantage:

- Little information is better than none.
- You can tell your competitor's next move by studying him.
- The more relevant information you have, the better you are prepared.
- Use the tools you have access to (and there are more than you think).
- Be creative in your approach when looking for information.
- Leave no doubt what knowledge about your competitors that is important to you.
- There is no excuse for not knowing your competitors.
- Make your own "competitor intelligence system".
- Outline/decide who is in charge of your company's intelligence gathering.
- Share your company's knowledge with all relevant employees! Discuss it as a group. Listen to what your employees think.

Only when you have mapped your competitors are you able to finish your own strategy.

THE TENTH COMPETENCE
EXPLOIT SET-PIECE SITUATIONS

We all have our favourites. Juninho, Ronaldino, Ronaldo, Beckham or maybe Roberto Carlos. All of them are among the best in the world when it comes to set-piece situations.

Few things in football are more impressive than the small group of world-class technical players who are able with extreme precision to pass the defensive wall, outplay the goalkeeper or pass the ball to an available striker with inch-perfect accuracy. We often remember these set-piece situations several years after we saw the actual match. What football fan can forget Beckham's goal against Greece on October 6th, 2001. England, needing a tie to qualify for the 2002 World Cup was trailing by one goal. With only seconds to spare in the game England receives a free kick approximately 7 metres outside the Greek penalty box. With great precision and power, Beckham scores one of the most beautiful goals ever for the English national team, so securing the team's participation in the 2002 World Cup.

The facts about set-piece situations

Every professional football player knows that set pieces win football matches. During the 2002 World Cup in South Korea and Japan, almost half of all goals were scored either directly or indirectly from set pieces – a total of 78 goals, including penalties. The figures were more or less the same during the 2000 European Championship.[57]

If we look at all World Cup finals from 1966-2002, a total of 16 out of 33 goals were the direct or indirect result of set pieces. Another five goals were the result of losing the ball in a set-piece situation but immediately recapturing it.[58]

Today, set pieces are obviously an essential tool for the professional football team. Not only is the execution of set pieces rigorously trained and rehearsed – many managers also train players in special combinations and moves that increase the chance of getting into set-piece situations in the first place. In this respect set-piece situations are a vital part of both the manager and the team's preparations, and set-piece variations are analysed in depth in the lead-up to important matches.

Why are set-piece situations decisive?

There are clear parallels in the business world for the application of set pieces. However, before going into these, let us consider *why* they are so decisive in the game of football.

In the book *Basic Team Coaching* published by the FA, the characteristics of a set-piece situation are described:

- *Ball possession*: The team that has been granted the set-piece initiative obviously has full control of the ball at the start of the set piece.
- *Restricted opposition*: Less opposition from the other team as the opponents need to keep at a distance until the ball is in play.
- *Mobilisation of additional resources*. The team that carries out the set piece can let additional players join the attack.
- *Training:* The team with the ball can execute a previously rehearsed situation.[59]

What we as business leaders need to ask ourselves is: What is the equivalent of the set-piece situation in business? And how can we exploit them to maximum advantage?

It would be interesting if you, as a business leader, could plan your business strategy with the aim of getting as many set-piece situations as possible. Taking the analogy further, you could then systematically prepare your team to get the most out of the set-piece situations you are able to generate.

Are there set-piece situations in the world of business?

Set-piece situations do occur in the world of business. But unlike in the football world, there is no referee using his whistle and pointing at the penalty spot. Set-piece situations in the world of business are much harder to spot and plan for.

Often it will come down to taking advantage of temporary windows of opportunity – for example, on the launch of a new product which has significant competitive advantages in the marketplace. In this case, you would say that the company has a "window of opportunity" until the competition manages to develop a similar product.

We are confident that set-piece situations happen in all trades and almost all companies. Unlike in the world of football it may not be the result of an opponent being penalised, but it could be a certain market situation, a specific new piece of legislation from the government or perhaps recurring business cycles that can be exploited in the same way.

A "translation" of a set-piece situation into business language could go like this:

- *Ball possession:* Your company has taken the initiative. It may have achieved unique market insight or been better at forecasting market developments.
- *Restricted opposition:* There is less opposition from competitors as they may have overlooked opportunities or perhaps face operational constraints in terms of weaker distribution systems, slower product development, loss of key personnel and the like.
- *Mobilisation of additional resources:* Your company has the opportunity to allocate resources directed at the specific situation in order to better take advantage of it.
- *Training:* Your company is able to train staff in specific procedures designed to address certain anticipated business opportunities as they arise.

There are numerous examples of companies which, for one reason or another, have been able to seize the initiative by following these principles. We see it often within product development, which also gives a "first mover" advantage. Examples could be:

- Pfizer's invention of Viagra
- 3M's invention of the Post-it Note
- Sony's invention of the Walkman

In all three cases these companies took the initiative with little or only slight opposition from competitors who were unable to field a similar product. Once these companies had taken the lead, they were able to mobilise additional resources and develop plans and procedures to take advantage of further product development opportunities.

Another example of "set piece" planning is FedEx, who made it their business to anticipate what others might regard as "unpredictable" situations.

Fedex's mission of delivering packages any place on earth has proved a success a long time ago. "Delivery on time" is one of the most important competitive criteria in this sector. There are endless things which may go wrong in the safe delivery of a product from, for example, Copenhagen to Lima.

FedEx had indeed learnt through experience that there will in fact always be problems on the route between Copenhagen and Lima. So they have turned the unpredictability to their advantage by becoming extremely flexible. They have created a global system that uses intelligence to help foresee when the "unforeseeable" situations will happen.

FedEx's Global Operations Control is based at the company's Memphis headquarters. This department's goal is to make sure that millions of packages are delivered on time – day in, day out – no matter what challenges FedEx might face. And there are quite a few. The Global Operations Control staff monitors everything from global weather conditions to political turbulence, strikes and gasoline shortages.

On a daily basis, there are local or regional factors that need to be taken into consideration and planned. During 2004 alone, contingency plans in connection with 37 tropical storms were outlined. In addition to this there are possible strikes, power failures, local gasoline shortages and much, much more.

This meant that FedEx was prepared several days in advance when tropical storm Katrina hit New Orleans in 2005. During the days before the storm, FedEx was able to gather and strategically distribute 30,000 bags of ice, about 140,000 litres of water, 85 power generators and four building repair equipment sets weighing two tons each. FedEx also managed to gather and send 60 tons of material on behalf of the American Red Cross.

The company's Global Operations Control means that FedEx, unlike many competitors, is able to foresee and take advantage of the weather, political turmoil, strikes and so on.[60]

For or against!

It is never certain who will get the next set-piece opportunity, whether this will be your own organisation or your competitors. In football, it often happens when strikers challenge defenders with deep runs toward the goal area, or when they try to dribble past the last defender. The challenging part is that the opponent's strikers will try to do exactly the same against your own defence.

This means that the planning of set-piece situations should consist of both "attack plans" and "defence plans".

A company should develop "offensive plans" as well as "defensive plans"

Since the world of business does not have a referee who can stop the game and decide to give one team a free kick against the other, in business it is not always clear who stands to gain and who stands to lose from set-piece situations. Whether a particular event may be to your advantage or disadvantage will depend, amongst other things, on the degree of preparation for the event, and whether or not you wish to react to it.

An interesting example from the world of business in Denmark was the government's decision to reduce excise duties on alcohol as of 1 October 2003. Not all companies were well-prepared for this new market situation. Therefore, a situation that at first sight looks similar to all can become both an advantage and a disadvantage.

In order to determine if a situation is an advantage or a disadvantage, as a business leader you should always look at the following checklist:

Category	Useful questions
1. Intelligence	Can the specific situation be foreseen? What happens right before the situation occurs?
2. Interconnected reasons	Is there a pattern of events? Do they occur between certain intervals?
3. Evaluation	Is the situation an advantage to the company? Is the situation a disadvantage to the company?
4. Action	Should the company react to the situation? Will the company gain from provoking the situation? Can competitors provoke the situation? How will competitors react in the given situation?
5. Response	Can the competition's next move be foreseen? Will the competitors act as they normally do?

In the military, all planning begins with intelligence. Intelligence is not the same as analysis. Contrary to analysis, the purpose of intelligence is to identify things or situations that occur prior to a certain event. In other words we are talking interconnected reasons that can be described over time. If "A" happens today, then "B" will happen tomorrow. By doing this, you have time for preparation and can better take the situation into account. But what the intelligence is based on differs a lot.

During the Vietnam War, the Americans found out that radio communication among the North Vietnamese units increased significantly just before an attack by the North Vietnamese. In order to better predict these attacks, the American air force dropped a large number of listening devices into the Vietnamese jungle.

You should also consider if the specific situation and perhaps the interconnected reasons can be taken advantage of actively, or if you should only prepare for the situation in a passive way. In order to complete this evaluation it is important to consider what the competition's move will be. Will the competitors trigger the situation themselves? And do they have a response available?

Two sectors often characterised by price wars are the gasoline and telecoms markets. In both markets, companies will benefit from planning what to do during a potential price war. They have to try to figure out if price wars in general are an advantage to them, whether to adopt a reactive "defence" plan, or whether they should initiate the price war themselves.

Set-piece situations and contingency plans

Since set-piece situations in the world of football come in many different shapes and forms, it is important to approach the issue in a systematic way. Instinctively you may think that you need to have a plan read for each specific situation. But that is not always possible.

In both football and the world of business, the challenging thing is that situations do not always happen exactly the way you had hoped.

In the world of football this is evident if for example the free kick you have been granted is further away from the goal than you have practised, or if the opponents mark in an unexpected way. The same challenges go for the world of business. It might be distribution not doing as you had planned, a competitor launching a new product or the occurrence of a price war.

But there are a number of techniques within strategic planning and scenario planning that are very common in the military and in professional football.

For example, a manager will benefit from having several basic strategies in place that he can use in different situations. In the end, it is about identifying groups of situations with the same features. Situations that have resemblances can be attacked or defended using the same plan. This is a huge advantage when planning. Instead of creating 10 plans for 10 different situations, the company may be able to deal with all situations using just three plans. This makes preparation and implementation much simpler. The advantages of simple systems have been described in the fourth competence of this book, "Make your strategy flexible".

The important thing is for the business leader to be aware which situations he should react to. In order to achieve this, he must first identify all the known situations that the company can expect to encounter, based on past history. These are situations the company will have direct experience of, and there will be plenty of detailed supporting information within the company.

The business leader must then try to identify the situations that *might* occur and may be important to the company. A useful technique doing this could be asking questions such as: "What if...?" or looking at comparable situations in other business sectors. Often these situations cannot be described in detail, since the company has yet to meet them.

A company should consider two types of situations: known and frequently recurring situations and unknown and rare situations.

When all the possible situations have been described, they are evaluated using two key factors: first of all, how likely the situation is to occur, and secondly how big an impact will it have on the company? The situations are placed in a chart with the two parameters as axes.

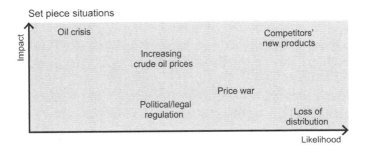

Next the events are grouped according to common characteristics. It could, for example, be that the oil crisis and political/legal regulation may be addressed the same way. They are both external factors and will affect all competitors equally. Rising crude oil prices and a price war could both put the company's revenue margins under pressure. New products launched by competitors and the loss of distribution will in both cases lead to loss of sales.

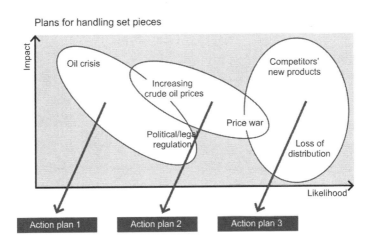

In business, as in the world of football, action plans are developed based on particular groups of situations or scenarios. This gives the manager a number of options. He can himself decide if he wants to react when a specific situation occurs. He can also choose to take the initiative and try to provoke a specific situation himself. For example, as we have mentioned earlier, he can decide to begin developing new products or start a price war if it seems to be an advantage.

In our experience, a business leader may have four different basic positions on specific situations:

- *Defend:* He is prepared, and has allocated sufficient resources.
- *Ignore:* The situation is not dangerous or there is only a slight chance it may occur.
- *Attack:* He allocates resources and provokes the situation himself.
- *Preventive attack:* He allocates resources and attacks in order to prevent a situation from occurring.

One company that is highly regarded in this area is America's Home Depot.

Home Depot was one of the best prepared companies when tropical storm Katrina struck New Orleans. They had already managed to relocate the families of their employees out of the danger zone, extra personnel had been deployed, all stores had been protected and additional equipment moved into position. The day after the storm, Home Depot was able to open 23 out of 33 stores in the disaster area. Within a week, all but four were back to business.[61]

Home Depot's success was not due to the fact that they had worked on a specific scenario called "Tropical storm in New Orleans". Rather, they had prepared for a range of contingent possibilities such as "breakdown of infrastructure", "damaged stores" or "evacuation of employees". Having developed plans for each headline contingency, they were equipped to draw on all or parts of the plans to deal with a variety of different situations, including hurricane Katrina.

Conclusion

Virtually all companies within all sectors can benefit from adopting "set-piece" strategies comparable to those exhibited in the world of football – both as a defensive and an offensive tool.

As a business leader you can get an advantage using the following key points:

- Take advantage of set-piece situations – they can mean the difference between victory and defeat.
- Identify the set-piece situations that are important to your company.
- Evaluate each situation based on importance and risk.
- Divide situations with the same features into groups.
- Create a contingency plan.
- Assess your options: *Defend, Ignore, Attack* or *Preventive attack*.

Companies such as FedEx and Home Depot are a great source of inspiration. The fact is that proper exploitation of set-piece situations can bring tremendous advantages.

EPILOGUE

Writing *Management by Football* has been a great challenge.

Over the three years it took to research and write the book it became apparent to us that there were two major obstacles we had to overcome.

The first obstacle we had to overcome was the lack of a solid frame of reference to start from. Many books have been written about sports psychology, sports strategy, biographies and so forth, but only very few books on the management skills of professional football managers. We quickly discovered that the most interesting element of a professional manager's job is not his personal management style, but rather what it takes to get the job done. Management style is often dictated by situation and is only one tool amongst many. We found that management style did not in itself describe the difference between football managers and business managers. Rather the difference lies in the football manager's constant and relentless focus on achieving a specific behaviour or performance.

The second obstacle we faced was that many of the best football managers have developed their own management skills and tools. They take decisions based on intuition and personal experience and it is often very difficult for them to explain exactly what they do and how they do it. This challenge is well known in the business world, where a great deal of research has been done in identifying best practice in companies. Best practice is often executed by individuals who are guided by instinct and who have become best performers precisely because they do not follow the rules and are able find effective management short cuts. Therefore, we have had to interview numerous people close to professional football managers such as assistant managers and key players. From a research standpoint this has also become a great advantage, as many of them have worked under several managers in different clubs. In this respect, they have been able to identify and describe the differences between various managers for whom they have worked.

We are very grateful for the many managers, players, journalists and researchers who have been generous enough to help and inspire us. As many of them have pointed out to us, the study of professional football managers is still in many ways uncharted water. The world of football and its hyper-competition holds a wealth of inspiration and best practices just waiting to be explored and described.

It has been very important to us that the publication of *Management by Football* is not seen as the end to a long process, but rather the beginning of something new and inspiring. We plan to continue researching, testing and exploring the concept of Management by Football. We will continue to work to identify ways to implement best practices, write up white papers and develop management tools. As part of our ongoing research project we have already tested more than 300 business managers on the 10 competences.

We have made this test available for you on our home page (see details below), and it asks all the vital questions you need to answer to become a better and more effective manager. In addition, we have started a Facebook group where we will continuously make available new research, tools and discussions.

We are always available for questions, comments or if you have a management experience you would like to share with us.

On a final note we hope that you have been as inspired by the professional football managers as we have and hope that you will be successful in your pursuit of becoming a top manager.

Go for gold.

Peter Boris Kreilgaard: peter@management-by-football.com
Henrik Aage Sørens: henrik@management-by-football.com
Daniel Kim Soren: daniel@management-by-football.com

www: management-by-football.com
Facebook: Management by Football
Twitter: http://twitter.com/managementfoot

REFERENCES

1 Erik Johnsen in Ledelse og erhvervsøkonomi, vol. 66. no. 4, 2002.

2 "Return on Leadership". Analysis by the Copenhagen Business School and Stig Jørgensen & Partners.

3 Rolf Jensen: Heartstorm [on the cover of "The Dream Society 2"], Viby J.: Jyllands-Postens Erhvervsbogklub, 2002.

4 www.uefa.com, 13 July 2007.

5 www.forza.dk, 17 June 2007.

6 www.sportenkort.dk 17 June 2007. www.forza.dk and www.thesun.co.uk 20 September 2007.

7 Telephone interview 16 January 2007.

8 "Kun plads til få store fodboldklubber", Børsen Business 24 March 2007.

9 e-mail interview.

10 Berlingske Tidende, 2 August 2007.

11 www.uefa.com, 21 September 2007.

12 Jack Welch: Straight from the Gut, New York: Warner Books Publishing, 2001.

13 David A. Vise: The Google Story, New York: Pan Books, 2006.

14 www.leoburnett.com.

15 Peter Kenyon: The Blue Revolution – Chelsea. The Movie. DVD, 2007.

16 David Meek and Alex Ferguson: A Will to Win: The Manager's Diary, London: Andre Deutsch Ltd., 1997.

17 David Meek and Alex Ferguson: A Will to Win: The Manager's Diary, London: Andre Deutsch Ltd., 1997.

18 The Official FA Guide to Basic Team Coaching, London: Hodder & Stoughton, 2004.

19 Private training, Lazio, February 2008.

20 Michael Hammer & James Champy: Reengineering the Corporation: A Manifesto for Business Revolution, London: Nicholas Brealey Publishing Ltd., 2001.

21 Jorrit Smink: Ajax Training Sessions, Reedswain, 2004.

22 BT, 6 November 2007.

23 en.wikipedia.org/wiki/Cristiano_Ronaldo.

24 en.wikipedia.org/wiki/Ruud_van_Nistelrooy.

25 Author of the book: Built to Last: Successful Habits of Visionary Companies, New York: Random House, 2005.

26 Jim Collins: Good to Great, New York: Random House Business Books, 2001.

27 Mentioned in Berlingske Tidende, Business 13 February 2008.

28 Interview with Arsene Wenger from UEFA DVD-Series, 2005.

29 Goal, February 2008.

30 Berlingske Tidende, Sport section 18 March 2008.

31 Carl von Clausewitz: Vom Kriege: Hinterlassenes Werk des Generals Carl von Clausewitz. Vollständige Ausgabe im Urtext, Bildungsverlag Eins, 2003. There is a shortened Danish version: Om krig: the central passages are in vol. 1-3, København: Rhodos 1986. Particularly regarding development of company strategy there is Thia von Ghyczy, Christopher Bassford and Bolko von Oetinger: Clausewitz on Strategy. Inspiration and Insight from a Master Strategist. New York: Wiley 2001.

32 Interview with Arsene Wenger from UEFA DVD-Series, 2005.

33 Jens Bangsbo, University of Copenhagen, former assistant manager of Juventus 2001-2004.

34 ProZone – Fatigue Study. February 2008.

35 Jim Loehr and Tony Schwartz: "The Making of a Corporate Athlete", Harvard Business Review, January 2001.

36 John Whitemore: Coaching på jobbet. En praktisk vejledning i at udvikle dine egne og dine medarbejderes færdigheder. København: Industriens Forlag, 1996, p. 19.

37 Eric Parsloe: The Manager as Coach and Mentor, London: Chartered Institute of Personnel and Development, 1999.

38 "Coaching Analysen 2005", by The Coaching Company, Copenhagen Business School, Civil-økonomerne, DJØF, IDA, Human Consult, PID and Enalyzer.

39 John Whitmore: Coaching på jobbet, page 68.

40 Paul Hersey and Kenneth H. Blanchard: Management of Organizational Behaviour: Utilizing Human Resources. New York: Prentice-Hall, 1986.

41 www.worldcoccer.com, 13 December 2007.

42 Steven Gerrard: My Autobiography, London: Bantam Press, 2006, p. 164.

43 John Whitemore: Coaching på jobbet. En praktisk vejledning i at udvikle dine egne og dine medarbejderes færdigheder. Copenhagen: Industriens Forlag, 1996. P. 30.

44 Patrick Barclay: Mourinho – Anatomy of a Winner, London: Orion, 2006, p. 139.

45 Patrick Barclay: Mourinho – Anatomy of a Winner, London: Orion, 2006, p. 140.

46 Patrick Barclay: Mourinho – Anatomy of a Winner, London: Orion, 2006, p. 141.

47 Frederick Herzberg, "One More Time, How Do You Motivate Employees?",Harvard Business Review Sep/Oct 1987

48 Carl von Clausewitz: Vom Kriege: Hinterlassenes Werk des Generals Carl von Clausewitz. Vollständige Ausgabe im Urtext, Bildungsverlag Eins, 2003. There is a shortened Danish version: Om krig: de centrale afsnit bd. 1-3, København: Rhodos 1986. Particularly regarding development of company strategy there is Thia von Ghyczy, Christopher Bassford and Bolko von Oetinger: Clausewitz on Strategy. Inspiration and Insight from a Master Strategist. New York: Wiley 2001.

49 Al Ries & Jack Trout: Marketing Warfare, 20. edition. New York: McGraw-Hill Professional, 2005.

50 Luis Lourenco and José Mourinho: José Mourinho, Made in Portugal – The Authorised Biography, Stockport: Dewi Lewis Media Ltd, 2004, p. 213.

51 Luis Lourenco and José Mourinho: José Mourinho, Made in Portugal – The Authorised Biography, Stockport: Dewi Lewis Media Ltd, 2004, p. 96.

52 UEFA Newsletter for Coaches. October 2006.

53 www.independent.co.uk 27 October 2005.

54 Interview with Peter Bonde 26 February 2008.

55 Paco Lloret: Rafa Benitez: The Authorised Biography. Stockport: Dewi Lewis Media Ltd., 2005. p. 193.

56 Philip Kotler: Marketing Management London: Pearson Education, 2002.

57 The Official FA Guide to Basic Team Coaching, London: Hodder & Stoughton, 2004.

58 The Official FA Guide to Basic Team Coaching, London: Hodder & Stoughton, 2004.

59 The Official FA Guide to Basic Team Coaching, London: Hodder & Stoughton, 2004.

60 Fortune Magazine, vol. 152, no. 7.

61 Fortune Magazine, vol. 152, no. 7.

ACKNOWLEDGEMENTS

We could not have written this book without the help of a large group of people who have contributed with experiences and viewpoints. In particular, we would like to thank you the following people:

- Thomas Helveg, OB (former Milan, Udinese and Inter player and Danish team captain).

- Andy Roxburgh, Technical Director, UEFA (among other things former manager of the Scottish national team).

- S.S. Lazio, Italian Serie A club (a big thank you goes to the team and the team "behind the team" for granting access to a private training session).

- Martin Jol, Head Coach, Hamburger SV (previously manager of clubs such as Tottenham Hotspur. Manager of the year in the Netherlands in 2001 and 2002).

- Jens Bangsbo, cand.scient. (Physical coach for the Danish national team and former assistant manager and physical coach in Juventus).

- Ebbe Sand (former player for Brøndby IF, Schalke 04 and the Danish national team. Striker coach for the Danish national team).

- John Peacock, Head of Coaching, the FA (former player and manager of several English national youth teams).

- Søren Lerby, player agent (former Ajax Amsterdam, PSV Eindhoven, Bayern Munich and the Danish national team player. Former manager of Bayern Munich).

- Allan Smith, football expert and journalist, The Daily Telegraph (former Arsenal and English national team player).

- John Sivebæk, player agent (former Manchester United, AS Saint-Etienne, AS Monaco and Danish national team player).
- Peter Bonde, assistant manager of the Danish national team, DBU (has played and managed several Danish clubs).
- Per Frimann, expert commentator (former RSC Anderlecht and Danish national team player).
- Peter Rudbæk, Technical Director, DBU (former manager of clubs such as AaB. "Manager of the Year" twice).
- Kim Vilfort, talent manager, Brøndby IF (former Brøndby IF, Lille and Danish national team Member).
- Jesper Jørgensen, director, Deloitte A/S (among other things responsible for Annual Review of Football Finance).
- Lars Olsen, chief manager, OB (former Brøndby IF, Trabzonspor, FC Basel and Danish national team player. "Manager of the Year" 2006).
- Barry McNeill, director, ProZone Sports Ltd. (world's leading company within products that analyse matches and player performance).
- Patrick Barclay, football expert and journalist (has covered six World Cups and seven European Championships for the Sunday Telegraph, EPSN and others. Author of Mourinho: Anatomy of a Winner).
- Graham Mackrell, Administration Manager, League Managers Association (an association of all Premier League and Football League managers).
- Birger Peitersen, football expert (former manager of Brøndby IF and others).
- Jonas Hebo Rasmussen (player for Arsenal's under 18 team).
- Morten Wieghorst, first manager of FC Nordsjælland (former Celtic and Danish national team player).

- Rakesh Sondhi, Managing Director, BMC Global Services Ltd (international strategy and management consultant. Specialises in using experiences from sports in management development).
- Børge Bach, Commercial Director, Royal League A/S (former managing director of AaB).
- Morten Bruun, expert commentator (former Silkeborg IF and Danish national team player and former manager of SønderjyskE and Silkeborg IF).
- Lynge Jakobsen, sports director, AaB.
- Sid Lowe, football expert and journalist, The Guardian (has in the last six years written about Spanish football for, among others, The Guardian, World Soccer and The Telegraph).
- Poul Hansen, expert commentator, TV 2 Sport ("Manager of the Year" 1999).
- Paco Lloret, Head of Sport, Camp Nou TV (author of for instance Rafa Benítez the authorised biography).
- Scott Campbell, director, Scott/Campbell A/S.
- Marcus Schmidt, senior lecturer, Copenhagen Business School.
- Palle Andersen, senior advisor, Catinet A/S.

INDEX

In his book, *Coaching for Performance*, John Whitmore describes the coaching process in terms of the following four-phase process, using the aptly derived "GROW" acronym:

- **G**oal – determination of the actual coaching goal.
- **R**eality – determination of the world in which the subject of the coaching is.
- **O**ptions – what options can the person being coached use?
- **W**ill – who has to do what and when?[39]

This may lead you towards a slight variation on the 6-point process described earlier, but the basic dynamic is the same. Always remember that it is the coach's responsibility to control the conversation in such a way that the person being coached touches all aspects of the chosen subject and finds their own solution to the problem. This is done by keeping focus on asking questions and disregarding your own opinions and solutions.

Although the coaching tool is relatively simple to use, and the advantages are obvious, surprisingly few business leaders actively use coaching in their organisations. Many managers prefer a more instructive method of training. However the two approaches are not mutually exclusive. It is possible to offer instructional training *and* one-to-one coaching in the same organisation, and those that do will vouch for the benefits.

Coaching and situational management

As we have seen, coaching is a powerful management tool, but it is important to recognise that it may not *always* be appropriate in *every* management context. This will depend to a great extent on what kind of employees you have and what their job functions are. In some cases a more instructional style of management may be required.

Whilst the development of staff is obviously important, it is also important to get the job done, and sometimes this may require more authoritarian action.

In order to get the job done, we create the frame of reference for the performance of the task, determining what is to be done, who we want to do it, and when we expect the job to be completed. This form of communication is very one-way.

On the other hand, in determining the way in which the task is to be performed, we focus more on the particular qualities of the person who has to perform the task. We seek to maximise their potential, enhance their performance, and develop them as "human resources", to ensure that the company has the best possible human production facility.

The interaction between the job-focus and personnel-focus has been systemised using the term "situational management". This theory was developed in 1969 by Paul Hersey and Kenneth Blanchard.[40]

Situational management

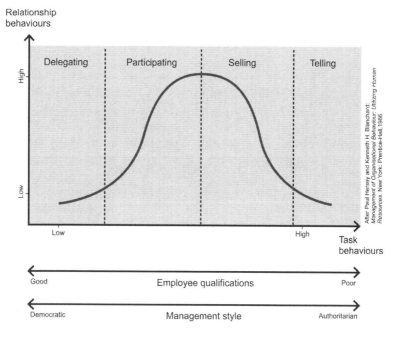

THE THIRD COMPETENCE
TURN STRATEGY INTO BEHAVIOUR

On 10 April 2007, a highly motivated Manchester United side played hosts to AS Roma at Old Trafford in the Champion's League group stage. AS Roma had won the first match 2-1 at home ground, and both teams knew that the result of the match would decide who would go on to the knockout phase.

Neither Manchester United's **Sir Alex Ferguson** nor AS Roma's **Luciano Spalletti** had any idea the match would turn into one of the most spectacular in Champions League history. At the end of the day, the home team had won 7-1.

The result of the match is groundbreaking in many ways. First of all, there is rarely this large a goal difference between two such professional managers and teams. Secondly, Italian teams very rarely lose by such a huge goal difference. Italian teams have always had a reputation for cultivating and developing excellent defenders and defence systems.

The match between Manchester United and AS Roma is a clear example that all preparation and strategy in the end hinges on behaviour.

Two top professional managers such as Sir Alex Ferguson and Luciano Spalletti will always be well prepared ahead of an important match. But on this particular April night, Sir Alex Ferguson was the only one who had success turning his strategy and system into winning behaviour on the pitch.

Luciano Spalletti is most likely the only one who knows whether his strategy and system failed, or if his team had a collective breakdown. But the result is not to be challenged.

Strategy is behaviour

Strategy is behaviour. Nowhere is this more evident than in football.

What business leaders can learn from professional football managers is their way of turning strategy into specific action. If a manager has ensured a solid foundation of strategy and system, he can begin turning strategy into specific behaviour among the players.

The intense competition and great transparency of football management mean that professional managers have always sought every possible means of enhancing performance. Today's professional managers not only look at the physical and technical dimension, but also at things such as diet, psychology, personality, attitudes, attire, behaviour on and off the pitch and much more.

You are what you do...

When in the world of business we talk about strategy, implementation and processes, we very often talk in abstract terms. Many companies are incapable of turning strategy and goals into specific action. What kind of behaviour does it take to increase sales by 25 percent? What kind of behaviour is required to develop 10 percent more new products? What is the behaviour of a company which wants to be perceived as modern, service-minded and innovative?

Often, management faces the challenge that these abstract plans are impossible to explain to the individual employee. How on earth do I, as a member of the canteen staff, act to make sure we are "modern", "service-minded" and maybe "innovative"? At the very best, employees will give it a shot, but in most cases it turns out you can be "modern", "service-minded" and "innovative" in many different ways.

Football managers are extremely good at turning their strategies into action. They have long time ago had to acknowledge that "you are what you do". The transformation of strategy into action in the world of professional football differs from that of most companies in that it is very physical and practical.